Corruption, Mafia Pow Italian Soccer

Whilst corruption and organised crime have been widely researched, they have not yet been specifically linked to sport. *Corruption, Mafia Power and Italian Soccer* offers an original insight into this new research area. Adopting a psycho-social approach based mainly on Pierre Bourdieu's praxeology, the book demonstrates that corruption and the mafia presence in Italian soccer reflect the Italian socio-political and economic system itself.

Supported by interviews with security agency officials, anticorruption organisations and antimafia organisations, and analysing empirical data obtained from a case study of 'Operation Dirty Soccer', this important study explains why mafia groups are involved in soccer, what the links are to political corruption and what might be done to control the problem. It also examines the mechanisms that make it possible for mafia groups and affiliates to enter the football industry and discusses how mafia groups exploit and corrupt Italian football.

This is important reading for undergraduate and postgraduate students, researchers and academics working in the areas of sociology, criminology, policing, anthropology, the sociology of sport, sport deviance, sport management and organised crime. It is also a valuable resource for practitioners in the football industry.

Alberto Testa is Associate Professor in Criminology at the University of West London, UK, and a visiting Senior Research Fellow at the SportcomLab of the University of Bologna, Italy.

Anna Sergi is Lecturer in Criminology and Deputy Director of the Centre for Criminology at the University of Essex, UK. She is an International Visiting Fellow at the University of Melbourne, Australia, and Chair of the Early Career Researchers Network of the British Society of Criminology.

Routledge Research in Sport, Culture and Society

Rethinking Olympic Legacy
Vassil Girginov

Surfing, Sex, Genders and Sexualities
Edited by lisahunter

The Aesthetics, Poetics, and Rhetoric of Soccer
Edited by Ridvan Askin, Catherine Diederich and Aline Bieri

Politics and Identity in Chinese Martial Arts
Lu Zhouxiang

Corruption, Mafia Power and Italian Soccer
Alberto Testa and Anna Sergi

Researching Difference in Sport and Physical Activity
Edited by Richard Medcalf and Chris Mackintosh

Surfing and Sustainability
Gregory Borne

Women, Sport and Exercise in the Asia-Pacific Region
Domination, Resistance, Accommodation
Gyozo Molnar, Sara N. Amin and Yoko Kanemasu

For more information about this series, please visit:
www.routledge.com/sport/series/RRSCS

Corruption, Mafia Power and Italian Soccer

Alberto Testa and Anna Sergi

Taylor & Francis Group
LONDON AND NEW YORK

First published 2018 by Routledge

2 Park Square, Milton Park, Abingdon, Oxfordshire OX14 4RN

52 Vanderbilt Avenue, New York, NY 10017

Routledge is an imprint of the Taylor & Francis Group, an informa business

First issued in paperback 2019

Copyright © 2018 Alberto Testa and Anna Sergi

The right of Alberto Testa and Anna Sergi to be identified as authors of this work has been asserted by them in accordance with sections 77 and 78 of the Copyright, Designs and Patents Act 1988.

All rights reserved. No part of this book may be reprinted or reproduced or utilised in any form or by any electronic, mechanical, or other means, now known or hereafter invented, including photocopying and recording, or in any information storage or retrieval system, without permission in writing from the publishers.

Notice:
Product or corporate names may be trademarks or registered trademarks, and are used only for identification and explanation without intent to infringe.

British Library Cataloguing-in-Publication Data
A catalogue record for this book is available from the British Library

Library of Congress Cataloging-in-Publication Data
A catalog record for this book has been requested

ISBN: 978-1-138-28993-2 (hbk)
ISBN: 978-0-367-89623-2 (pbk)

Typeset in Perpetua
by Apex CoVantage, LLC

To my Franco and Giovanna with love.

—Alberto Testa

A mamma Teresa, papà Lullo ed Elida.

—Anna Sergi

Contents

Foreword viii
Acknowledgements by Alberto Testa and Anna Sergi xi

1 Introduction 1

2 Corruption, mafia and the Italian power 'field': a Bourdieuian analysis 18

3 Scandals, the 'sins' and 'sinners' of Italian soccer 57

4 Hidden power: the 'Calcio' mafia style 83

5 'Ndrangheta and 'Dirty Soccer' 116

6 Conclusion – mafia and Italian soccer: the state of the game 143

Index 161

Foreword

Until relatively recently, corruption and organised crime were usually treated as discrete entities. For instance, the UN adopted its Convention against Transnational Organized Crime in 2000 – symbolically, in Palermo – and a quite separate Convention against Corruption in 2003. Fortunately, an increasing number of states and international organisations now realise that organised crime and corruption are often closely intertwined: awareness of the overlaps and linkages is vital if these negative phenomena are to be adequately countered.

Another fairly recent development is the broadening of the definition of corruption to cover not only public officers but also 'entrusted' power-holders in the private sector – and even in sport. While the World Bank for decades preferred the narrow definition of corruption that required that a public official be involved, it has since 2017 begun to use the broader approach that had been adopted many years earlier by agencies such as the world's leading anti-corruption nongovernmental operation (NGO), Transparency International. Thus, it is now normal to refer to corruption in FIFA, for example, whereas misconduct in a body of that sort would in the past usually have been labelled – certainly by specialists – according to its specific nature (e.g. bribery, embezzlement, money laundering, etc.).

Much of this change relates to the global spread of neo-liberalism, which blurs the boundaries between the public and private sectors. Increasingly, authorities, the mass media and members of the general public realise that corruption can be found far beyond the public sector and that the boundaries between corruption and organised crime have become ever more hazy. It is thus highly appropriate that Alberto Testa and Anna Sergi provide us in this simultaneously fascinating and disturbing book with a prime example of the ways in which organised crime and corruption interact and overlap.

It is also very fitting that the case study they explore so thoroughly is primarily based in Italy. While criminologists often draw a distinction between organised crime and mafia (the latter being a specific variant of the former), many journalists and ordinary members of the public use the terms interchangeably – although the true mafia originates from Italy's most southerly region, Sicily. In this book, the authors also explore the role of two of Italy's other crime syndicates, the Naples-based camorra and in particular the Calabrian 'ndrangheta, in corruption. Italy is also the home of one of the best-known cases of mass political corruption, the so-called *Tangentopoli* scandal of the early-1990s – and of a man that some have alleged is the most corrupt West European leader of recent decades, Silvio Berlusconi.

But Italy is not only a prime example of a country with high levels of organised crime and – certainly by European standards – corruption: it is also home to one of the world's leading soccer teams. The Italian national team has won the FIFA World Cup no fewer than four times: only Brazil has won it more (five times). Quite simply, football (*calcio*) is by far the most popular sport in Italy, as well as globally – and Italians love to bet on it. This is an obvious target for organised crime and corrupt officials.

Given the confluence of these various factors, the following analysis is timely – the soccer scandal on which it is based emerged only in May 2015 – relevant and significant. The study uses an approach based primarily on the ideas of French social theorist Pierre Bourdieu, as well as on psychoanalytic and social capital theories. But it is also empirical, using both judicial documents and other data generated by 'Operation Dirty Soccer', as well as interviews with key actors.

While the principal aim of the study is to demonstrate the close connections between organised crime groups, corrupt officials and soccer teams, it also has an applied public policy dimension. Thus, Testa and Sergi show how the policy change of the early twenty-first century that permitted Italians to bet on the result of a single soccer match greatly facilitated match-fixing, thus playing into the hands of organised crime groups and corrupt officials. They also show how the internet is a two-edged sword: while it has many positive attributes, it is also the case that online betting plays into the hands of organised crime. But Testa and Sergi do not only expose the reasons for what has already taken place: they also make concrete suggestions on how the problems they have analysed can be addressed. One important point they emphasise is that change must be initiated at the local level: a bottom-up approach is likely to be more effective than a top-down one, even though political will at the top is also vital.

The lessons Testa and Sergi draw from their analysis of the linkages between organised crime groups and corrupt officials in relation to soccer are applicable not only in other areas of Italian life but also elsewhere: Italy is in many ways a microcosm of what is, regrettably, happening all over the world. In this sense, their study is of significance way beyond the Italian borders.

Professor Emeritus Leslie Holmes, Fellow of the Academy of the Social Sciences in Australia at the University of Melbourne, an Expert of Transparency International and a member of the 'Anti-Corruption Practitioners' Network', United Nations Development Program Europe 2008.

Acknowledgements

This book originates from research conducted between 2015 and the present, so the acknowledgements necessarily reflect this long timeframe. This study would have not happened without the support of the Autorita' Nazionale Anticorruzione (Italian Anti-Corruption Authority–ANAC) and the Italian Ministry of the Interior. Specifically, I would like to thank Counsellor Michele Corradino (ANAC) for the patience in answering my questions (especially the silly ones!); Chief Constable Dott. Emanuele Ricifari for sharing his expertise and knowledge on the mafia phenomenon; and Deputy Chief Constable Dott. Marco Garofalo of the Italian Police for having shared with me their expertise on mafias, specifically the 'ndrangheta.

I would like to thank Rob Wainwright, executive director at Europol, for being immediately supportive and for having facilitated contacts with the Italian branch of the agency; in relation to this I would like to thank Dott. Francesco Stampacchia of the Direzione Centrale Anticrimine, Servizio Operativo Centrale–Polizia di Stato (Anti-Crime Central Directorate, Central Operational Service–SCO of the Italian police) and Chief Constable Dott. Paolo Sartori for the support giving me in 'navigating' the Italian security agencies landscape.

My gratitude also goes to Wolfgang Rahm, Kriminalhauptkommissar of the Landeskriminalamt Baden-Württemberg, Italienische Organisierte Kriminalität (Germany State Police); Dirk Herzbach, Koordinator deutsch-französische Polizei- und Zollzusammenarbeit Landeskriminalamt Baden-Württemberg (Germany State Police). I would like to thank Verbi Software for allowing me to use their qualitative data analysis software MAXQDA, crucial to making sense of the copious data obtained from the research interviews.

Without mentioning names for security reasons, I would also like to thank the Direzione Investigativa Antimafia (Antimafia Investigative Directorate) for their support, together with the Polizia Di Stato and other Italian security agencies (Carabinieri and Guardia di Finanza); they are the model for excellent practice in Europe in the prevention and fight against organised crime.

Sincere thanks are also due to Dott. Davide Del Monte, executive director of Transparency International-Italia, expert of corruption in the Italian context; Dott. Paolo Corbi of the Italian Football (soccer) Federation; and Dott. Giuseppe Monguidi of the Lega Calcio Serie B for answering my questions with precision and honesty.

Finally, a big grazie is also due to the Italian Antimafia Association Libera and specifically to Dott. Bruno Palermo and Dott. Fabio Giuliani for sharing their daily experience in contrasting the 'ndrangheta and camorra and helping me to make sense about the nexus fans-organised crime.

Last – but certainly not least! – I would like to acknowledge with gratitude the support of senior commissioning editor Simon Whitmore for giving us the opportunity to write this book and for his constant trust in the project, and my university (University of West London) for the support given to the book project.

As the book is about Italy, the country of Roman Catholicism, my acknowledgements could not end without thanking 'my Saints' Padre Pio, St Anthony and St Benedict, who have answered my prayers to see this work finally finished.

Alberto Testa

In addition to the previous acknowledgements, I would like to thank first and foremost the Direzione Distrettuale Antimafia (DDA, Antimafia District Directorate) in the city of Catanzaro, Calabria, Italy, for their support while collecting the judicial files for Operation Dirty Soccer. Special thanks in Catanzaro go to antimafia prosecutors Elio Romano and Giovanni Bombardieri for their engagement during our interviews and their availability.

Acknowledgements xiii

I am also grateful to antimafia prosecutor Alessandro Sorrentino for his support and his expertise in collecting documents in Catania, Sicily, for his availability and for sharing his expertise during our interview. Thank you also to antimafia prosecutor Michele Prestipino in Rome for an extremely lucid discussion on corruption in Italy and to Antimafia Prosecutor Paolo Toso for his support in the access of documents in Turin.

I am also thankful to Giuseppe Lumia with the ROS (Special Unit for Organised Crime within the Carabinieri force) for his never-ending informal support and his engagement with academic work.

Special thanks to Carlo Macrì, journalist and correspondent of *Il Corriere della Sera* for his help in retrieving documents in Calabria and his endless patience.

Finally, a qualitative work like this is the result of many different inputs, conversations, confrontations and discussions, which is very difficult to disentangle. Connie Agius, journalist with ABC; Pete Fussey, Nigel South and Anna Di Ronco, at the University of Essex; Luca Storti, at the University of Turin; and, last but not least, my father, Pantaleone Sergi, my mother, Teresa Papalia, my sister and my brother-in-law, Elida Sergi and Cleto Romantini, are among the many that I wish to thank for their patience, support and certainly inspiration.

Anna Sergi

—

Both authors wish to thank Emeritus Professor Leslie Holmes at the University of Melbourne for agreeing to write the foreword of this book and Professor Nicola Porro for the continuous support of this project.

Chapter 1

Introduction

In 2017, Italian media reported that two Italian and three Spanish men were arrested in Spain; this group comprised the coach, the assistant coach, the general manager (Nobile Capuani) and two Spanish players of the Eldense Soccer Club (Segunda B division). The coach was arrested for corruption, as the Eldense FC had allegedly 'adjusted' the match (by losing) with the Barcelona B team.

The Spanish authorities also investigated another five soccer matches involving Villareal B, Atletico Baleares and Cornella, because they suspected that the high amount of betting on these matches concealed match-fixing; the newspaper *El Confidencial* also pointed out that the 'ndrangheta, one of the most aggressive Italian mafia groups, was behind these episodes and suggested that it was trying to infiltrate Spanish soccer to strengthen the business of illegal betting derived from Asia.[1] The Italian newspaper *Corriere della Sera*[2] also reported that the former coach Mario Cartagena was replaced by the arrested coach, explaining:

> The Italians [Nobile Capuani's entourage] brought players who paid to play [to be included in the first team], but who were not skilful enough for our championship. He brought them here to Di Pierro [the arrested coach], they called them 'wire transfer' players.

The *Corriere della Sera* also argued that Capuani allegedly worked with the former soccer player Ercole Di Nicola, already allegedly involved in cases of illegal betting and match-fixing in Italy, particularly in a criminal operation alongside the 'ndrangheta.³ The Eldense FC case demonstrates that corruption and mafias⁴ are not only active in the Italian business and political systems but also emerge in very different socio-cultural practices such as soccer, and beyond Italian borders.

It is always unsettling for fans when the media report on the dark side of soccer. Violence, racism, doping and, most importantly, corruption are becoming common features of twenty-first-century soccer, and more widely, competitive sports. At first sight, this connection is counterintuitive.

Sport is one of the world's most popular social practices; since the era of ancient Greece, physical activity and sport have played a major part in youth education. Social scientists have stressed the importance of these activities; Dutch historian Johan Huizinga (1949) pointed out that the values of playing were among the most important human needs, emphasising the important connection between games and culture.

American sociologist Erving Goffman (1961) perceived games such as sport as an instrument of simulation – a symbolic location where individuals experienced social dynamics safely, without any effects on their real lives. Simulation is one of the game's traits; the other trait is the uncertainty of the result. As simulations, games allow individuals to reproduce and test socio-cultural aspects occurring in society without 'taking the fall'.

Sport is also a powerful symbol to make sense of numerous human experiences. For instance, individual and team sports such as soccer are both symbols of resilience. This resilience is captured when athletes show their spirit in suffering during important performances, often playing while injured; this metaphorically can be translated into the abilities of individuals to face life's adversities doing their best and to never give up. Sport, with its rules and values, also tends to promote ethical principles that are embodied in the concept of fair play, which reflects the ideals of honesty, dignity and respect for one's teammates, opponents and the referees during a competition (Loland, 2002).

However, with time, modern sport (and soccer) has gradually become an occupation and clearly reflects one of the most significant values of a modern society founded on capitalism. American sociologist James Coleman (1987) identified this value in what he terms 'the culture of competition', wherein being wealthy and successful are the main goals of human life.

The problem is that the culture of competition seems to play an important part in the diffusion of corruption-related practices, and this is true also for sport and ultimately for soccer. Huizinga (1949) identified a degeneration in the historical development of sport in its 'winning at any cost' logic. Huizinga's reasoning supports French sociologist Roger Caillois (2001 in Salvador),[5] who argued that games are reflections of human evolution, pointing out the socio-political and cultural transformations which are currently occurring or which have occurred in the past.

Soccer, the most popular sport in the world,[6] displays all the negative features explained earlier, including corruption, as the Eldense FC scandal symbolises. This scenario should not surprise; sport, as Eitzen (2006) argued, "is not a sanctuary . . . corruption, law breaking, unethical behaviour and other crimes are endemic to human societies" (p. 8). Eitzen's statement is certainly suitable to describe the origin and the current state of affairs of soccer in Italy (Cf. Spaaiji and Testa, 2016; Testa and Armstrong, 2010; Testa, 2013), where soccer not only tends to reflect the extensiveness of corruption-related practices in Italian society but also underlines the important role played by the mafias in the evolution of this country (Lodato, 2012).

A recent project by Transparency International – the Corruption in Sport Initiative[7] – advocates for keeping sport clean as a global imperative. In 2017, this organisation issued a report titled 'Agenda Anticorruzione'[8] (Anti-Corruption Agenda), which positions Italy, a G7 member, the third-largest economy in the Eurozone and the eighth-largest economy in the world, in 60th place out of 176 countries in the Corruption Perception Index ranking list (which ranks countries in relation to their perception levels of corruption). Within the European ranking, Italy is the third highest, with only Greece and Bulgaria ranking higher.

That mafias and corruption go together is not new (Ruggiero and Gounev, 2012), but the severity and pervasiveness of this problem has reached new heights. In 2017, the Italian media reported[9] that an immigration centre located in Calabria, in a location called Island of Capo Rizzuto – which hosted 1,500 migrants and was considered to be the largest reception facility in Europe – was allegedly infiltrated by the clans of the 'ndrangheta. 'Operation Johnny' saw among the arrested Leonardo Sacco, governor of the 'Fraternity of Mercy', the organisation that managed the centre. The operation uncovered a network which was led by a 'white collar' of the 'ndrangheta clan 'Arena' that managed public procurement and supply contracts linked to the Prefecture (central government institution on a county level). According to the investigation, of over € 100 million allocated to the immigration centre, at least € 30 million was sent to the 'ndrangheta clan.

Operation Johnny caused media uproar because the police also arrested Padre Edoardo Scordio, a local parish priest, with a charge of mafia association and the accusation of having facilitated the movement of the funds to the 'ndrangheta clan. The operation had uncovered a corrupt 'system of power' aimed mainly at exploiting immigrants and refugees by profiting on managing immigration centres and the money provided to fund them by the local, national and European authorities.

Operation Johnny not only confirmed the pervasiveness of Italy's crime syndicates, as the link to 'ndrangheta and local church showed (Dalla Chiesa, 2015), but also how systemic corruption is crucial for mafias to operate in the country (Ruggiero, 2010; Ruggiero and Gounev, 2012). The operation is a clear example of when individualistic explanations of corruption, frequent in literature (cf. Rose-Ackerman, 1978; Klitgaard, 1988), do not capture the phenomenon in its entirety, certainly not in the Italian context. As argued by Ruggiero (2010), in Italy "corruption has played the function of a foundational conduct, one that lends itself to be imitated" (p. 103), therefore becoming a system.

When institutions appear corrupted, when corruption appears to become the 'rule of the game', when it becomes so worrying that the president of the Italian Republic Sergio Mattarella in 2015 called upon the nation to fight the widespread corruption and the mafia groups,[10] it makes little sense to dwell on why a person is willing to risk his or her job or reputation to obtain some sort of advantage.

Within this social context, one should not, therefore, be surprised that soccer in Italy, with its recurrent scandals and with the amount of money that it generates, would become a centre of corruption and a thriving business for the mafia groups. Padre Luigi Sturzo – a Sicilian priest and one of the founding fathers of the Italian Christian democratic party – was the first politician to point out the pervasiveness of the mafia, arguing:

> The mafia clamps in its tentacles justice, police, administration, politics; the mafia that today serves to be served tomorrow, protects to be protected, penetrates into the ministerial cabinets, in the corridors of Montecitorio [Italian Parliament], pursues secrets, seeks documents, forces men believed to be honest to [commit] dishonourable and violent acts. It is the scary revelation of Italy's moral 'pollution', it is the wretched wounds of our country.[11]

Mafias certainly find fertile ground in soccer to reinforce their power. In 2012, *Sport Radar*, the world leader in sports data analysis, listed Italy second in its ranking (of 53 countries) for corruption in soccer in relation to match-fixing, which is one – albeit not the sole – criminal activity that involves mafia clans. The Italian police and all the country's security agencies, always at the forefront of the fight against the mafias, have a clear idea about their involvement in soccer. In 2017, the Italian Chief of the Police, Prefetto Franco Gabrielli, stated:[12] "Crime groups see in the goal economy an opportunity to expand illicit trafficking as well as their power in the social fabric." Gabrielli points out the two main reasons (which will be explored in this book) why the mafias are 'playing' soccer – namely money, but also social consensus and prestige, hence control of the territory where they operate. The latter is somewhat overlooked by academic analyses, but crucial to make sense of the mafia-soccer link. It is the same mechanism as the one behind the reason why mafia fugitives are often captured in the region where their clans operate. Deputy Chief Constable 'G' of the Central Directorate Anti-Crime (Italian Police) underlines how significant this dynamic is to explain the mafias and especially the Calabrian 'ndrangheta logic:

> Having successful fugitives shows that the clans are able to protect their members; it shows their capillary control of the territory. And the strong social consensus [. . .] that fugitives can escape arrest for

several years also shows that in some territories the major value of the mafia '*omertà*' [code of silence] and population's attitudes – in the form of non-cooperation with authorities and non-interference with illegal behaviours of others – are quite strong. For the fugitives, being free is also a power test, especially if they can hide where their clans operate.[13]

Fabio Giuliani, exponent of the Campania region section of Libera (Italian antimafia charity) and soccer fan, argued:

> Knowing the phenomenon of organised crime in Campania, I can safely state that the crime syndicates are interested in any licit and illicit business; the camorra [Campania region mafia] try to infiltrate soccer because it is an important means to create social consensus and access powerful social networks at local and national levels.[14]

'*Il calcio*', as a popular and institutionalised social practice, has historically mirrored the political and social conditions and issues present in the country (Testa, 2013), so it is not surprising that the 'tentacles' of the mafias are clamping it.

Structure of the book

This book reflects the first scholarly investigation on corruption in Italian soccer, focusing on the role that the mafias play in this important socio-cultural practice, and originates from the spirit of sharing, collaboration and mutual learning between Alberto Testa and Anna Sergi.

Alberto Testa has researched and published widely on soccer and its 'darker sides', focusing also on far-right activism and violence since 2007. His theoretical approach is psycho-social in nature, informed by Bourdieu's praxeology but also by (neuro-)psychoanalytical theory, especially the role of the unconscious in making sense of social behaviour.

Anna Sergi has widely researched and published on organised crime and particularly on the notorious Calabrian mafia 'ndrangheta; her research approach is socio-legal in nature, mostly on the behavioural aspects of criminal networks and on emerging complex structures of power and alternative or concurrent governance styles.

The chapters of the book are the result of cross-contamination of these research backgrounds. Testa primarily but not exclusively has focused on the overall theoretical frame of the book, as well as chapters 2 and 3, while Sergi has focused primarily but not exclusively on chapters 4 and 5.

Departing from literature in both corruption studies and mafia studies, the analysis is supported by the use of empirical fieldwork data obtained after (and during) the recent 'Operation Dirty Soccer', an investigation carried out primarily by the Direzione Distrettuale Antimafia (Antimafia District Directorate) in Catanzaro, Calabria, and which afterwards moved to other antimafia offices in the country. In particular, the authors were granted access to the judicial documents of the investigation and conducted interviews with the prosecutors in charge of the operation.

The Italian soccer scandal came to light in May 2015 when the antimafia prosecutors of Catanzaro decided to investigate match-fixing involving soccer clubs of the Lega Pro and Serie D (the third and fourth tiers of Italian soccer, respectively); 70 people were investigated and 50 arrested, with a total of 30 soccer clubs involved. This scandal is representative for three main reasons: firstly, the authorities were able to understand and describe the involvement of the 'ndrangheta clans in the soccer business; secondly, prosecutors uncovered a 'system' of corruption similar to those the Italian authorities and media uncover almost daily involving the country's local and national power systems; thirdly, because the investigation has involved in its latest developments the Lega Serie B (second division), thus showing the national reach of mafias' influence in Italian soccer.

As mentioned earlier, soccer does not exist in a social vacuum. Chapter 2 will, therefore, contextualise soccer within the Italian 'social space', starting from a premise that corruption and mafia are the two sides of the country's power system coin and that it is unfruitful to neglect corruption in any analysis that focuses on Italian mafia. Corruption functions as the bridge between mafias and the Italian power system at a local and national level – corruption-related practices in Italy are serial and diffused (Davigo, 2017).

The chapter will start by reviewing the literature on corruption and mafia generally and within the Italian 'anomic' context. Both phenomena are difficult to define – corruption in particular because it refers to the changes in the country's socio-cultural, economic and political domains. Chapter 2 will also introduce the book's theoretical framework, which is psycho-social in orientation, drawing mainly but not exclusively from Pierre Bourdieu's praxeology (1999), which focuses on the reciprocal influence among social actors, environments and social relations by integrating individual 'strategies', motives, constraints and influences originating from social structures (Reay, 2015). The book's theoretical framework also emphasises unconscious processes in making sense of society and social phenomena, so it has an 'applied psychoanalytical' element; in this it is in-line with Alligham's argument that individuals are – at least in part – linked together in what can be defined as 'unconscious contracts'. Unconscious motives and processes are not only important in understanding individuals' behaviour but repeated and consistent (deviant) social practices.[15]

Corruption as a social phenomenon displays specific major traits: according to Alatas (1990), it requires that more than one individual is involved and linked in the exchange of benefits and reciprocal obligations. It involves the deception of public and private organisations and communities, or the society as a whole. In soccer, for instance, a referee can ask for money because he/she has the power to do so; this potentiality is already gratifying regardless of the positive (profit) or negative (sanction) of the illicit act.

In chapter 2 and the rest of the book, we also differentiate the term 'corruption', as a logic, from corruption-related practices – any behaviour which is informed by this logic. This is in line with the psycho-social theoretical lens of the book which sees the individual mind as a location where the psychological and the social merge.

Finally, chapter 2 will focus on the role that mafias have played in Italy, with particular attention given to the Calabrian 'ndrangheta clans, while not failing to overlook the Sicilian cosa nostra and the Neapolitan camorra, all active in Italian, and some cases European, soccer. Corruption, mafias (and of course soccer) meet precisely when and where crime groups seek to exploit power or become powerful through corrupt practices. Mafia groups, as stated by Vannucci (2010), are governance actors that can and will exchange corrupt practices. This book will show that soccer, which is both a tool for promoting social consensus (especially at local and regional levels) and a profitable business, offers a perfect example of a social 'field' in which power control is sought by wealthy and well-connected criminals, corrupt(ible) entrepreneurs and/or local politicians (Sergi, 2015).

Chapter 3 will discuss the wider topic of Italian soccer and corruption, focusing on its numerous 'scandals'. Scandals have sociological significance; they violate the 'sacred', which represent the collective and regulate traditional social relations; they should provoke a strong collective reaction – they are moments of Durkheimian collective.

From a Bourdieuian perspective, scandals are a means to reveal the moral fabric of a 'field' and more widely of a social space to assess if the collective has become indifferent to the transgressed norms (De Dampierre, mentioned by Kantola and Vesa, 2013). Italian corruption scandals, along with their impacts and diffusion in several fields of the Italian 'social space', seem to confirm the public perception on corruption and mafia cases as non-scandals and a *de facto* situation where these two social phenomena are acknowledged as part of the country's power system. Hence, chapter 3 will evaluate the main soccer scandals. Italian soccer is one of the most successful in the world; however, this 'pedigree' has been tainted by a history of scandals which consistently – since 1927 (Vignati, 2016) – have been reported by the Italian media. Finally, the chapter will identify the main forms of corruption in soccer by highlighting how corruption cases in soccer tend to reflect the same sophistication and seriality occurring in other domains of the country's power system.

Chapter 4 will focus on the role that mafia groups have historically played in Italian soccer, examining how mafias exploit the weaknesses of Italian soccer in order to seek social consensus and maintain the control of their territories. The chapter will offer an analysis of various instances in which mafia groups have interfered in the control and running of soccer teams and clubs at both national and local levels and will focus mainly, but not exclusively, on illegal betting and match-fixing; it will also hint at the dangerous connections between some Ultras (hard-core fans) groups and mafia clans (Testa, 2018[16]). The chapter will also analyse instances involving the Lega Serie A (Italian Premiere league division) teams and some soccer players to discuss how mafia power influences soccer not just through access to merchandising, services and teams but also through key soccer players and sport personalities.

Chapter 5 will focus on the case study of 'Operation Dirty Soccer' by presenting a qualitative analysis of its judicial documents, which include wiretaps from the Italian public prosecution and the presentation of the evidence gathered. The chapter will provide a historical framework of the investigation and will mainly look at what can be learned and confirmed through this operation. Operation Dirty Soccer represents an ideal case study (a) to demonstrate how investigations in the local strength of mafia power lead to capturing the interference of mafia groups in social practices such as soccer and (b) to consider how the reputation of mafia groups, together with a systemic corruption network, can indeed supersede the local. With growing attention on the way, the Calabrian mafia is socially embedded in the reality of the Calabria region as well as across Italy and abroad, and it becomes crucial to look at the way the clans nourish social consensus as well as play their roles in their communities, also via soccer and corruption-related practices. Chapter 5 will end by demonstrating the importance of considering corruption as embedded in mafia behaviour; the more mafia clans are embedded in their communities, the more fluid corruption becomes.

The final chapter of the book concludes the discussion by focusing on the practical implications of this work. It is evident from the book's analysis that corruption and mafia presence in soccer is not an exception in a contrarily virtuous Italian socio-political and economic system. Therefore, it is inconceivable that Italian soccer should be left unchanged; it is in need of a profound reform, a reform which considers all the players and the interests involved. The chapter will summarise the findings and discuss strategies of prevention and 'containment' of mafia activities in Italian soccer. Realistically, we can identify only containment and prevention as being feasible strategies to combat mafia activities in soccer, and although the Italian state has achieved numerous successes against different mafia groups, mafia power today remains to be defeated, as it is a very complex social phenomenon which predates Italy's unification (1871) – it affects the country as a whole and not just its southern regions anymore.

Methodological notes

This qualitative study is based on three research strategies. It first draws from French sociologist Pierre Bourdieu's social theory. The premise on which the book is based is that to understand social action, it is important to consider the objective structures that compose the social world while at the same time not neglecting the subjective lives of individuals, which are always informed consciously or unconsciously by a pragmatic calculation of profit.

Hence, the book essentially has a psycho-social conceptual framework aiming "to understand the mutual effectivity of psychological and social realms in the production of identity, action and relating" (Hollway, 2006, p. 15). This framework was used prior to data collection and after our literature review as the 'scaffolding' of the study, creating "categories"[17] and "descriptors" used in the coding process (Owen, 2014, p. 7).

Qualitative research is necessarily exploratory, fluid and flexible, and certainly context-dependent (Mason, 2002). The main questions that were addressed in this study are the following:

- Why do mafia clans seem to be increasingly involved in Italian soccer?
- What is the link, if any, between the country's power system and mafia clans in the context of soccer?
- What are the mechanisms that make it possible for mafia clans and affiliates to enter the soccer industry?
- How do mafias exploit and corrupt Italian soccer, and what can be done to contain the problem?

These research questions require first and foremost an understanding of key concepts at the basis of the analysis, which is why the book dedicates two chapters to criminological concepts such as mafia and corruption first before consequently applying these contexts to soccer.

12 Introduction

Our second strategy focused on data collection from documents such as governmental directives, laws, sentencing examples and debates listed in socio-legal periodicals and in the Italian media. German sociologist Max Weber was the first to underscore the importance of documents in social research, as society and the world at large are shaped via writing and documents (Weber, Roth and Wittich, 1978); language, regardless of whether it is written or spoken, represents power dynamics and politics (Bourdieu, 1993) – the fundamentals of the human mind can be found in language (Lacan, 1997). Hence, document analyses help to uncover meanings and enhance understanding of social problems investigated.

As for the purposes of qualitative research (Blaikie, 2000; Bachman and Shutt, 2011), interviews have allowed exploration in a more efficient way of the practicalities of investigations and procedures. The interviews have been carried out mostly through purposive and strategic sampling, considering that the research covers specific fields where experts are not that numerous and need to be targeted specifically. The interviews were carried out at different times by both authors during two trips each to Italy and include both discussions on mafia and corruption and/or directly on mafia groups' involvement in soccer practices. A list of organisations (in no particular order) which either have contributed to the interviewing process or provided documental data is provided here.

> Autorità Nazionale Anticorruzione (Italian Anti-Corruption Agency)
> Ministero degli Interni (Ministry of the Interior) Direzione Centrale Anticrimine (Central Directorate Anti-Crime)
> Polizia di stato (Italian Police), Servizio Centrale Operativo (Central Operative Service-SCO)
> Direzione Investigativa Antimafia (Italian Antimafia Investigative Directorate)
> Lega Serie B
> Transparency International-Italia
> Libera (Antimafia Association; Campania section)
> Direzione Distrettuale Antimafia (District Antimafia Directorate – DDA), Catanzaro (Calabria) unit

Direzione Distrettuale Antimafia (District Antimafia Directorate – DDA), Reggio Calabria (Calabria) unit

Direzione Distrettuale Antimafia (District Antimafia Directorate – DDA), Catania (Sicily) unit

Guardia di Finanza (Italian Financial Police)

Europol, The Hague: Top Serious Organised Crime unit

Landeskriminalamt Baden-Württemberg; Italienische Organisierte Kriminalität Stuttgart (State Criminal Police; Italian Organised Crime Unit)

As the purpose of this book is to combine various perspectives about different fields of enquiry, the research has been carried out at various times to expand the field of investigation and follow the evolution of concepts and their intertwining (Marvasti, 2004). In essence, this research has been largely based on a combination of textual data from official sources, such as investigations and wiretap transcripts and/or official reports, in addition to formal and informal interviews conducted with key players in the investigation and in the field of interest more generally.

All the interviews have been carried out with multiple interests in mind. First and foremost, interviews with experts in a field, specifically targeted for their expertise, "can serve to shorten time-consuming data gathering processes, particularly if the experts are seen as 'crystallisation points' for practical insider knowledge" (Bogner et al., 2009, p. 2). Secondly, the interviews, even though explorative in nature, have been "conversations with a purpose" (Burgess, 1984, p. 202), as they aimed to understand not just the problem but also some parts of the solution to the problem. Nevertheless, the conversations have been kept quite loose and without a proper structure to allow participants free flow of thought. Certainly, the importance of mixing documents and interviews is linked to the ideology of constructing a more dynamic, interactive and up-to-date picture of the research field at hand. Indeed, the initial approach to data has been an interactive one, to allow all the material to come together as it was collected, to construct themes, understand contexts and discourses.

Our last research strategy involves a 'directed content analysis' using the qualitative data analysis software MAXQDA. Applying the theoretical framework to categorise prior research, we identified significant notions and variables and used them as initial coding groups (Hsieh and Shannon, 2005; Potter and Levine-Donnerstein, 1999); subsequently, operational definitions for each category were determined using the theory. When data did not fit the coding categories, they were examined to determine whether they could fit an existing category as a subgroup or form part of a new category.[18]

As our analysis is based on investigations and judicial work and often prompted by investigative journalistic efforts, too, it has been necessary to operate through critical analysis a thorough questioning of what often has been presented as 'the truth' in documents or in interviews. Indeed, especially in crime-related subjects of complexity, like this one, the picture presented by the data collected has needed interpretation and deep study of all the components involved. This means, for example, that even though our analysis has focused on the different and many relationships in soccer – among whom are soccer players, mafia clans and corrupted politicians or entrepreneurs – the contexts in which these relationships operate present diverse geographical, social, cultural and economic features that need to be considered, even if only at the background of the analysis.[19]

Notes

1 Cf. www.elconfidencial.com/espana/2017-04-04/12-0-eldense-barcelona-mafia-calabresa-futbol-ndrangheta_1360198/
2 Cf. www.corriere.it/sport/17_aprile_05/eldense-l-ombra-ndrangheta-almeno-altre-cinque-gare-sospette-ae0340bc-19e0-11e7-988d-d7c20f1197f1.shtml?refresh_ce-cp
3 Ercole di Nicola was arrested during operation "Dirty Soccer". The Eldense FC case is not a one off instance about the link soccer-mafias; currently (the 24th of May 2018), the Italian magistrates of the city of Bologna have requested a sentence of six years of imprisonment for the former Juventus FC and Italian World Cup-winner national team player Vincenzo Iaquinta for his alleged involvement with the 'ndrangheta (Calabria region mafia). http://www.

sportmediaset.mediaset.it/calcio/calcio/-ndrangheta-chiesti-6-anni-di-carcere-per-vincenzo-iaquinta_1215506-201802a.shtml; cf. Chapter 5.
4 'Mafias' is the plural for mafia, and in this book indicates the three major regional criminal syndicates in Italy, namely, cosa nostra (Sicily), camorra (Campania), 'ndrangheta (Calabria).
5 Cf. https://tesionline.unicatt.it/bitstream/10280/1993/1/Tesiphd_Completa_Salvador.pdf
6 Cf. www.tpi.it/2015/10/02/mappa-sport-popolari/
7 Cf. http://transparency.org/news/feature/sport_integrity
8 Cf. www.transparency.it/wp-content/uploads/2017/10/Agenda-Anticorruzione-2017.pdf
9 Cf. www.liberoquotidiano.it/news/italia/12384847/ndrangheta-immigrati-cara-isola-capo-rizzuto-fondi-europei-68-arresti-don-edoardo-scordio.html; www.quotidianodelsud.it/calabria/cronache/giudiziaria/2017/10/25/operazione-jonny-esce-carcere-don-edoardo-scordio-concessi
10 Cf. www.ilfattoquotidiano.it/2015/02/03/giuramento-mattarella-presidente-montecitorio-larbitro-essere-imparziale-diretta/1392306/
11 Luigi Sturzo in *La Croce di Costantino* (January 21, 1900), mentioned by *L'Osservatore Romano*, the newspaper of the Vatican City; www.osservatoreromano.va/it/news/riarmo-morale
12 Cf. www.calcioefinanza.it/2017/05/03/gabrielli-calcio-antimafia/
13 Excerpt 16 interview G (2017); in our interview, Garofalo rightly points out at the end that sooner or later the police close in and will arrest the fugitives; for this reason, now fugitives tend to escape abroad.
14 Excerpt 5 interview BP (2017).
15 Cf. Allingham, M. (1987). *Unconscious Contracts*. London: Routledge.
16 Testa, A. (2018). 'The All-Seeing Eye of State Surveillance in the Italian Football (Soccer) Terraces: The Case Study of the Football Fan Card'. *Surveillance & Society* 16(1): 69–83.
17 The categories used reflect concepts such as Habitus, field, Doxa, power, 'capitals' and reflexivity.
18 An audit trail was implemented to promote research accountability and a neutral free research process.
19 In this book we will refer to people involved, to different degrees, in judicial enquiries. Some of these investigations are concluded; some others are not or never have gone beyond the investigation stage; some individual positions are still pending and awaiting conclusive trials. Everyone mentioned in this book who has not been convicted by a court of law, obviously, shall be considered innocent until proven guilty. The aims of this book are strictly analytical and shall not be intended as evaluation or judgement of civil or criminal

responsibility at any stage. Even when we name individuals, the reader shall always assume we refer to investigations, but these investigations are solely used for the purposes of analysis and research and do not, at any stage, substitute for the sovereignty of a court of law.

References

Alatas, S.H., 1990. *Corruption: Its Nature, Causes and Functions*. London: Aldershot.
Allingham, M., 1987. *Unconscious Contracts*. London: Routledge.
Bachman, R.D. and Shutt, R.K., 2011. *The Practice of Research in Criminology and Criminal Justice*. London: Sage.
Blaikie, N., 2000. *Designing Social Research*. Cambridge: Polity.
Bogner, A., Littig, B. and Menz, W., 2009. *Interviewing Experts*. Basingstoke: Palgrave Macmillan.
Bourdieu, P., 1993. *Language and Symbolic Power*. Cambridge, MA: Harvard University Press.
Bourdieu, P., 1999. *On Television*. New York: New Press.
Burgess, R.G., 1984. *In the Fields: An Introduction to Field Research*. London: Allen and Unwin.
Caillois, R., 2001. *Man, Play and Games*. Carbondale: University of Illinois Press.
Coleman, J.W., 1987. Toward an Integrated Theory of White-Collar Crime. *The American Journal of Sociology*, 93(2), pp. 406–439.
Dalla Chiesa, N., 2015. A proposito di Mafia Capitale. Alcuni Problemi Teorici. *CROSS. Rivista di Studi e Ricerche sulla Criminalità Organizzata*, 1(2).
Dalla Chiesa, N., 2010. *La convergenza. Mafia e politica nella Seconda Repubblica*. Milano: Melampo.
Davigo, P., 2017. *Il sistema della corruzione*. Milano: Laterza.
Durkheim, E., 1982. *The Rules of Sociological Method and Selected Texts on Sociology and Its Method*. New York: Free Press.
Eitzen, D.S., 2006. *Fair and Foul: Beyond the Myths and Paradoxes of Sport*. Lanham, MD: Rowan and Littlefield.
Goffman, E., 1961. *Encounters: Two Studies in the Sociology of Interaction*. Indianapolis, IN: Bobbs-Merrill.
Hollway, W. (2006). *The Capacity to Care: Gender and Ethical Subjectivity*. London: Routledge.
Hsieh, H. and Shannon, S., 2005. Three Approaches to Qualitative Content Analysis. *Qualitative Health Research*, 15(9), pp. 1277–1288.
Huizinga, J., 1949. *Homo Ludens: A Study of the Play-Element in Culture*. (R.F.C. Hull, Trans.). London: Routledge & Kegan Paul
Kantola, A. and Vesa, J., 2013. Mediated Scandals as Social Dramas: Transforming the Moral Order in Finland. *Acta Sociologica*, 56(4), pp. 295–308.

Klitgaard, R., 1988. *Controlling Corruption*. Berkeley: University of California Press.

Lacan, J., 1997. *The Language of the Self: The Function of Language in Psychoanalysis*. Baltimore, MD: John Hopkins University Press.

Lodato, S., 2012. *Quarant'anni di mafia: Storia di una guerra infinita*. Milano: BUR Biblioteca University Rizzoli.

Loland, S., 2002. *Fair Play in Sport: A Moral Norm System*. London: Routledge.

Marvasti, A., 2004. *Qualitative Research in Sociology*. London: Sage.

Mason, J., 2002. *Qualitative Researching*. London: Sage.

Owen, G., 2014. Qualitative Methods in Higher Education Policy Analysis: Using Interviews and Document Analysis: The Qualitative Report, 19. Available: www.nova.edu/ssss/QR/QR19/owen52.pdf

Potter, W.J. and Levine-Donnerstein, D., 1999. Rethinking Validity and Reliability in Content Analysis. *Journal of Applied Communication Research*, 27, pp. 258–284.

Reay, D., 2015. Habitus and the Psychosocial: Bourdieu with Feelings. *Cambridge Journal of Education*, 45(1), pp. 9–23.

Rose-Ackerman, S., 1978. *Corruption: A Study in Political Economy*. New York: Academic Press.

Ruggiero, V., 2010. Who Corrupts Whom? A Criminal Eco-System Made in Italy. *Crime, Law and Social Change*, 54(1), pp. 87–105.

Ruggiero, V. and Gounev, P., 2012. *Corruption and Organized Crime in Europe: Illegal Partnerships*. London: Routledge.

Sergi, A., 2015. The Italian Anti-Mafia System between Practice and Symbolism: Evaluating Contemporary Views on the Italian Structure Model against Organized Crime. *Policing*, 10(3), pp. 194–205.

Spaaiji, R. and Testa, A., eds., 2016. *Hooliganism*. Routledge International Handbooks edn. London: Routledge.

Testa, A., 2013. Normalization of the Exception: Issues and Controversies of the Italian Counter-Hooliganism Legislation. *Sport in Society*, 16(2), pp. 151–156.

Testa, A. and Armstrong, G., 2010. *Football, Fascism and Fandom: The Ultras of Italian Football*. London: A&C Black.

Vannucci, A., 2010. L' evoluzione della corruzione in Italia: evidenza empirica, fattori facilitanti, politiche di contrasto. Available: www.astrid-online.it/static/upload/protected/Vann/Vannucci.pdf [January 14, 2016].

Vignati, A., 2016. *Scandalo Calcio*. Milano: HOW2 Edizioni.

Weber, M., Roth, G. and Wittich, C., 1978. *Economy and Society: An Outline of Interpretive Sociology*. Berkeley, CA: University of California Press.

Chapter 2

Corruption, mafia and the Italian power 'field'
A Bourdieuian analysis

After the major corruption scandal 'Tangentopoli' (Bribesville)[1] in Italy in the '90s, many Italians hoped for a national political and moral renewal period, which would have stressed the transparency and accountability of the political system and its administration of the *res publica*. Reality has proved these hopes were mistaken; corrupt practices involving politicians, businesses and state bureaucrats are uncovered by the Italian judiciary almost daily.

Obviously, corruption is not a social phenomenon peculiar only to Italy; in 2016, former UK Prime Minister David Cameron stated, "Corruption is an enemy of progress and the root of so many of the world's problems" (*The Telegraph* – online, 2016). It is worth noticing that in the same year and one month prior to Cameron's speech, a major corruption scandal – this time in soccer – had affected the Fédération Internationale de Football (soccer) Association (FIFA): its former president, Sepp Blatter, was investigated by the Office of the Attorney General of Switzerland (OAG) on suspicion of criminal mismanagement and misappropriation.[2] Moreover, in 2015, 14 FIFA officials were arrested; the US attorney general who led the investigation stated: "They were expected to uphold the rules that keep soccer honest. Instead they corrupted the business of worldwide soccer to serve their interests and enrich themselves."[3]

So, as the earlier examples show, corruption does not stop at national borders nor involve only the political system of a country. However, in Italy, corruption has reached a substantial level of diffusion. To support this statement, it suffices to mention two relatively recent major scandals involving two Italian cities and their local political parties: in 2014, Italians found out that the Mose project, an investment to protect the city of Venice from flooding, was at the centre of a kickback system which saw 100 people investigated and 35 arrested. Among those involved were politicians who represented the current government and the opposition, businessmen and bureaucrats, including a former commander of the Guardia di Finanza (the Italian financial police, which often investigates cases of corruption). According to Judge Carlo Nordio, the uncovered criminal system was more complex and sophisticated than Tangentopoli.[4]

Two years later, in December 2016, was another major corruption scandal, this time involving the capital city of Rome and the newly elected Movimento Cinque Stelle (5 Stars Movement) administration. Notably, the M5S is the party which presents itself as an anti-establishment political player, fiercely opposing enduring Italian systemic corruption, a sort of Italian political moralization force. Although the newly elected mayor, Virginia Raggi, was not at the time of writing directly involved, her chief of personnel, Raffaele Marra, described by the media as a person with extraordinary influential power – and for this reason known by the nickname of Rasputin[5] – was charged and arrested because he allegedly demanded money from a businessman in exchange for public work contracts issued by Rome's city council.

In Italy, hence, corruption-related practices seem endemic; according to Italian anti-corruption expert and judge Piercamillo Davigo (2017), in Italy, corruption has not only become sophisticated but also serial and diffused.

It is in this social milieu – what French sociologist Pierre Bourdieu would identify as 'social space' – that the relationships between soccer, mafia and corruption must be understood. The aim of this chapter is to provide a snapshot of the Italian 'social space', where mafia meets a corruption-led Italian power system and mafia and corruption-related practices have become so preponderant as to result in an inevitable day-to-day recurrence for many Italians.

The chapter begins with a review of the literature focusing on the corruption and mafia phenomenon, then introduces the book's theoretical framework, which is psycho-social in nature and aims "to understand the mutual effectivity of psychological and social realms in the production of identity, action and relating" (Hollway, 2006, p. 15).

To achieve these intentions, we draw primarily but not exclusively from French sociologist Pierre Bourdieu's praxeology (1999), which in our opinion helps to understand the scale of the diffusion and tolerance of corrupt practices in twenty-first-century Italy as well as tolerance or even normalisation in some parts of the country of the mafia phenomenon. In doing so, the chapter will set the context for understanding corruption in Italian soccer and its links to the mafias. Finally, the chapter will examine Italian anti-corruption and antimafia strategies.

Making sense of corruption

Corruption is a multifaceted phenomenon whose complexity is proved by its many, and often competing, explanatory theories. Corruption practices differ according to individuals and organisations but also to cultural, political and economic variables. However, corruption, as we will see later in the chapter, must be understood essentially for its link to power. If power is the focus on analyses of corruption, the social dimension of this phenomenon becomes obvious. In this book we refer to corruption as "the intentional misperformance or neglect of a recognised duty, or the unwarranted exercise of power, with the motive of gaining some advantage more or less directly personal" (Brooks, 1909, p. 4).

This definition allows us to go beyond the Italian legal typology of corruption, which mainly focusses on corrupt practices committed by state officials, politicians and private citizens who deal with them, and to explore the variety of corruption-related practices that are reported daily by the Italian media.

Corruption in this book is intended as a logic – in Bourdieuian terms as one of the main '*doxa*' (the 'rules of the game') of the Italian power system. It is pervasive and influences social relationships and social exchanges in many different domains; in the higher education field, for instance, it may become evident when a president of an Italian university selection panel chooses an academic not because of his/her CV but because he was asked by a politician or the university's vice chancellor to do so in exchange for favours for his/her own career. In the soccer field, we may find a player who plays badly to make his team lose in order to favour illegal betting, or a soccer club president who pays a referee to 'adjust' the result of a match in order to gain prestige and social consensus in the city where the team is located and among hard-core soccer fans.

As Graaf[6] explains, corruption, similar to many other social phenomena, is analysed along the lines of the long-standing theoretical debate on agency vs structure. While agency stresses the freedom of the individual in relation to motivation and choice, suggesting that individuals are conscious of their acts even though they do not always know their consequences, structure refers to society and the external environment and how these influence individuals – individuals do not act completely on their own impulse: there are structural preconditions for their acts (Eriksen, 2015).

Pierre Bourdieu (2009) explains this dilemma, arguing: "The main division is the opposition between subjectivism and objectivism" (p. 56). The nature of this polarisation promotes several quandaries to address, and as Graaf[7] details, if the social structure influences individual behaviour, how does this process occur? And if agency is the predominant force, in which way does it create and change social structures?

According to the agency vs structure dichotomy, causal explanations of corruption may be classified in three major groups, namely rational choice approaches, structural/social approaches and relational models, the latter aiming to combine the two opposing points of analysis.

Rational choice explanations stress subjectivity, and they are largely based on a utilitarian view. Individuals become corrupted or corrupters because of a rational, conscious calculation of cost vs benefits – the cost and benefit produced by a corruptive practice, the likelihood of being punished and the severity of the sanction if the offender is caught are the main motivators.[8]

The rational choice approach tends to underplay structures' influence and individual past experiences. Its focus is directed to a conscious utility maximisation; the centrality of individuals is crucial in the explanation of collective outcomes (Carson, 2014). The problem of this explanation of corruptive practice dynamics is that it does not clarify why individuals in the same circumstances and having the same cost-benefit assessments might decide not to become corruptible or to corrupt, hence why they do not pursue their expected profits or tangible/symbolic rewards.

Structural/social theories provide several explanations of corrupt practices; social norms determine what is acceptable in society, and individuals are socialised to follow them to be part of society – their obedience is necessary. Studies have demonstrated that the link among social norms, compliance and corruption-led practices is that corruption seen as a norm is more likely to reoccur (Jansics, 2014).

As mentioned in chapter 1, Coleman (1987) instead focuses his analysis of corruption-related practices on the 'culture of competition' of capitalist societies. Success and becoming rich fast is so engrained in modern society that, in order to pursue these aims, people may consider illegitimate means; corruption becomes a possibility and a good way to climb the social ladder. This logic is evident in sport, controversially summarised by American football coach Vince Lombardi, who argued that in sport "Winning isn't everything. It's the only thing."[9]

Economics explanations point out how corruption-led practices depend on shared expectations. The cost and benefit of corruption-related practices depend on how diffused the behaviour is in the same society – if being corrupted or corrupting is expected, then being honest is not convenient. The more corruption is pervasive, the more agents are likely to comply to maximise their profit/interest (UK Department for International Development, 2015).

Corruption is perpetuated rationally and consciously because the agents who should control and eventually punish the offenders feel that their function will not succeed in changing the fact that many people are involved in corruptive exchanges anyway (Marquette and Peiffer, 2015).

Lack of control and the relationship between administrative devolution and corruption are also the focus of Fisman and Gatti's analysis (2002 in Di Nicola and Zanella, 2011), which highlighted that smaller countries tend to be less corrupted because they establish a strict ethical code in the public administration while controlling national and/or local politicians and bureaucrats more efficiently.

There is also a third stream of explanations of corruption which focuses on the social network dimension of the phenomenon.

The relational model focuses on an association across social actors to pursue profit (Jansics, 2014). As opposed to the rational choice approach, this interaction involves more than two actors – a network or web of participants. This model does not focus only on economic exchanges but also on other non-monetary mutually profitable exchanges such as favours, patronage and gifts. This model has the merit of capturing the complexity of corruption and attempting to bridge the gap between agency and structure. As Jansics (2014) noticed, these corrupt exchanges impact not only the social actors involved but also institutions and, more widely, society, promoting specific justifications for corruption-led behaviours, thus promoting their diffusion.

In relation to the Italian context, Vannucci (2010) argues that corruption can be explained by focusing on its political, social and economic roots. The most frequent causes mentioned by Vannucci are the lack of a clear contraposition and variation in power of opposing political forces (this promotes poor accountability and transparency); the high cost of doing politics and to maintain the political parties' system; the politicisation of the judicial system; a lack of tough legislation to punish political parties and politicians if corrupted; the inefficiencies of the bureaucratic apparatus at national, regional and local levels; and asymmetries in moral and civic culture in promoting the respect of the rule of law.

Regardless of theoretical differences, in order to understand corruption in Italy, it is crucial to focus on its peculiar trait, namely its seriality and wider diffusion – this data appears to indicate some kind of internalisation process within the Italian social space. For this reason, perhaps, it may be more fruitful to conceive corruption as a logic that has the potential to be internalised by social actors. In Italy, the diffusion and seriality of corruption-related practices is shown by the daily scandals uncovered by the media and investigated by the judiciary. The director of the Italian branch of Transparency International is very clear on this point:

> Corruption practices in Italy are not an emergency problem; they do not only occur once in a while. Corruption is a systemic issue, from the local public institutions to the national ones. This is not only my opinion; it is sufficient to read a newspaper – every day there is a scandal, ranging from major scandals [the previously mentioned Mose project in Venice] to micro cases, for instance the one involving a senior surgeon in Milan who broke bones just so he could fix them

afterwards. Normalization in relation to corruption [in Italy] means that corrupt practices can be found everywhere and at any moment.[10]

This severe but grounded analysis of the Italian context stresses not only a high level of normalisation and tolerance of corruption in the country but describes a fertile ground for the emergence, existence and perseverance of another long-standing Italian problem, the mafia phenomenon.

Mafia and mafias: a historical sketch

The word 'mafia' was originally used to describe the functioning of crime groups or clans in Sicily, but with time it has been used to describe all Italian crime groups in their regional manifestations. Amongst the most important are: cosa nostra (from Sicily), camorra (from Campania) and 'ndrangheta (from Calabria). Other groups, such as the Sacra Corona Unita in Puglia, the Famiglia Basilischi in Basilicata and the Banda della Magliana in the city of Rome, have emerged at different times, as a manifestation of the mafia 'problem' being a widespread form of organised crime in the country. Indeed, despite the many successes obtained by the Italian state, mafia power is still considered to be extremely strong and not just a 'problem' of the southern part of Italy.

In fact, the mafia 'problem' has widened progressively in other Italian regions; the north for example, which traditionally did not previously experience a strong mafia presence, seems to be the target of a process of 'colonisation' or 'transplantation' of mafia activities, or investments (Varese, 2011). Different mafia clans – particularly those from Calabria – have settled in the social fabric of northern and central Italian regions through a variety of illicit and licit enterprises (Sergi and Lavorgna, 2016).

In 2016, for instance, the police arrested 40 individuals in Calabria, Lazio and the northern region of Liguria with linkages to the 'ndrangheta (the official name of Calabrian mafia clans). Some of those arrested were in contact with local, regional and national Calabrian politicians as well as tax and revenue officers from the same territory.[11] This expansion drive from the southern region of Calabria to the northern regions has also been mirrored in soccer, as chapters 4 and 5 will underline.

As with corruption, the concept of 'mafia' is difficult to define, as it is a phenomenon that is in continued mutation, adapting to changes in the country's socio-political and economic milieu; indeed, this ability to remain an invisible yet influential and resilient power make it difficult to analyse it. A good start perhaps is to understand the connections of mafia within the concept of 'myth'. Myths, symbols and rituals are an enduring source of human inspiration, so it is not surprising that they are also linked to the genesis of mafia.

Social anthropologist Bronisław Kasper Malinowski (1926) argues that a myth is not just a story but "a reality lived . . . a living reality believed to have once happened in primeval times, and continuing ever since to influence the world and human destinies" (p. 81). Myths are used to justify and/or explain social practices and, most importantly, social and moral orders – providing them "antiquity, reality and sanctity" (p. 86) – and because of these traits, they can be a powerful justifier of human action and perception.

Cosa nostra,[12] camorra and 'ndrangheta origins are mythological, with the 'original' mythical account narrating that three Spanish knights, Osso, Mastrosso and Carcagnosso, members of a secret society called Gaurduna, supposedly moved to Italy in 1412 to escape justice, having defended the honour of their sister. The lore explains that they reached the island of Favignana in Sicily, and for 29 years they worked in secret, writing the rules of a powerful new secret organisation. Osso then remained in Sicily and founded the mafia, Mastrosso went to Campania and founded the camorra, and Carcagnosso went to Calabria and founded the 'ndrangheta (Ciconte, 2011). As myths also have a 'sacred' dimension, which is highly effective in achieving their functions (Malinowski, 1926[2015]), it is clear that this myth is no different – it also has a Christian dimension; Osso represents Jesus Christ, Mastrosso – St Michael, and Carcagnosso – St Peter (Lupo, 2011; Ciconte, 2011).

Cosa nostra – Sicily

Regardless of the mythical origin of the three mafia organisations, as explained earlier, the origin of the term 'mafia' is connected originally to Sicily and the ninth-century Arab invasion (Natella, 2002). Its etymology seems to be based on the Arab word Mahias – a bold man – or Ma Afir – the name of a Saracen tribe which ruled the city of Palermo (Hess, 1998). In 1862, the term 'mafia' was used for the first time in the theatre in the play 'I mafiusi di la Vicaria', which details life in the Palermo prison; the inmates (mafiosi) were described as 'uomini di rispetto' – honourable men (Di Bella, 1991). This portrait has been successfully used by the film industry and made popular by American director Francis Ford Coppola, when the second part of the *Godfather* story explains how Don Vito Corleone became a mafioso in America by killing a local gangster who was bullying the local population; for this he gained status as an honourable man, the man to contact in case of perceived injustice.

In 1865, a classified document signed by the prefect (local state representative) of Palermo mentions "Maffia, o associazione malandrinesca" (mafia or criminal organisation), and in 1871 the Italian police law refers to "lazy vagabonds, mafiosi, and suspicious individuals in general" (Lupo, 2011, p. 3).

In the early 1870s, many of the traits which define the modern Sicilian mafia phenomenon were already evident through analysis of the fast growth of the citrus fruit industry. Dickie (2004) mentions the story of Dr Gaspare Galati, who in 1872 inherited an estate which produced lemons and tangerines and who had to deal with a mafia-affiliated warden and his rich boss, Antonino Giannona. The story showed the perceived unreliability of the local police, the judiciary and fellow landowners when Galati decided to fight off the boss and his protection racket. It also outlines the mafia *modus operandi*: "protection rackets, murder, territorial dominance, competition and collaboration between gangs, and even a hint of a code of 'honour'" (p. 44) as well as one of the main elements through which mafia power in all its manifestations has allegedly prospered: the lack of trust of the population in the state and the perceived collusion between cosa nostra and local Italian state representatives (Gambetta, 1996).

The recent history of cosa nostra is characterised on the one hand by setbacks and significant defeats, often paid for with the lives of public servants (police officers, judges and politicians) killed to defend Italian democracy, and on the other hand by its evolution to become more adaptable to societal changes (Scalia, 2016). As the chief constable of the Italian Anti-Crime Central Directorate argues:

The Sicilian mafia prefers to blend into the economic, social and political domains (including secret societies such as the Masonic lodges) by using corruption as a bridge to interact with the political, economic and bureaucratic powers. The clans are involved in illegal activities such as drug trafficking, but they also run legit firms which operate in the business of public work contracts.[13]

As with the other forms of mafia, the power that the Sicilian cosa nostra exercises acts to control the territory illicitly via extortion or legitimately via electing politicians sympathetic to the clans. and local (and national) soccer are not neutral in regard to this strategy, as chapter 4 will show.

Camorra – Campania

The camorra (mafia in Italy's Campania region), at the time of writing, is enjoying worldwide infamy, and this time not only for its crimes and violence but because of the 'glamour' created by the TV crime drama *Gomorrah* – based on the book (and blockbuster movie) written by journalist Roberto Saviano (2011), aired in Europe by Sky Atlantic. In 2016, the British newspaper *The Guardian* described the drama as "unmissable . . . makes *The Godfather* look like [UK comedians] Gilbert and Sullivan".[14]

The etymology of the term 'camorra' is contested; according to Sales (1993), camorra was a term that referred to a form of gambling undertaken in the Neapolitan Kingdom since 1735, where a 'kumar' – Arab word for 'fee' – was to be paid to those who controlled the game to avoid violence. Camorra essentially means 'extortion' of money.

Barbagallo (2011) mentions the year 1860 as significant to learning more about the history of this mafia. He cites the Swiss writer, Marc Monnier, who in his works not only describes 1800s Neapolitan society but also the deprived suburbs of the city and how the camorra operated. The camorra in the 1800s was already involved in extortion, the majority of which was carried out inside prisons against other prisoners, but it also pervaded the outside, too.

The twenty-first-century camorra tends to be more fragmented in its overall structure (Gibilaro and Marcucci, 2005); it never had the hierarchical structure of cosa nostra or the quasi-governmental expression of both the Sicilian and Calabrian mafia groups, even though attempts of unification were made over the years. Without having such structure, it has always been considered less cohesive and more inclined to in-fighting and violence (Allum, 2016).

According to Dalla Chiesa (2012), while for cosa nostra, businesses and politics tend to be separate entities connected by a mutual exchange of favours and resources, with the camorra these three entities tend to coincide, a trait also shared with the Calabrian 'ndrangheta.

Indeed, the system of camorra conquers political influence in small and medium-sized towns, where it is easier to buy votes and to control not only local politicians but also bureaucrats and businessmen who in return help the clans, especially when the state issues public work tenders.

A significant example of the political protection that camorra enjoys and has enjoyed in the past is provided by the 'Cosentino's case'. In 2017, the antimafia prosecutors of the town of S. Maria Capua Vetere arrested and convicted for external participation to mafia association a former minister and senator for the Forza Italia party (former prime minister Silvio Berlusconi's party) Nicola Cosentino, who was considered by the public prosecutors as the national political protector of the Camorra Casalesi clan, one of the most powerful and well-connected clans at the national and international level.[15]

In terms of activities, the illegal businesses of camorra vary from drug trafficking to counterfeiting and, most worryingly, the disposal of toxic waste in Campania and other Italian regions, as recently confirmed by the camorra boss (and current witness of the prosecution) Nunzio Perrella.[16] The camorra is also active in legitimate public construction and waste management, and its members are becoming true stakeholders in the local governance. As Martone (2014) states:

> Camorra clans play an active role in the development of the territory by setting up consortia and by cooperating with local administrations. . . . They integrate into the local network of stakeholders

and social groups with their own local rules and regulations which, whether explicit or implicit, lay out the distribution of resources.

(p. 74)

'Ndrangheta – Calabria

When it comes to the Calabrian 'ndrangheta, the first mentions of its existence were in the documents of the Tribunal of Lamezia Terme in 1877; this mafia's origins can be found in the seventeenth-century struggle between the farmers and the landowners, the dominant class of the time in the Calabria region.[17]

The term 'ndrangheta probably originates from the union of the Greek words of 'Aner' and 'Agathos' which indicate valour and masculinity; the two words combined are similar to 'ndrangheta and indicate 'society of men of honour' (Ciconte, 2011; Gratteri et al., 2014). With time – as occurred with the term mafia and camorra – there was a shift between a positive to a negative meaning, indicating the 'ndrangheta as 'malandrineria' (rascals), yet this was still mitigated by the myth of a society of men of honour, a trait in common with the other syndicates (Ciconte, 2011) and justified by its mythological origins.

In 2007, the 'ndrangheta became known to the world for its ferocity; in Duisburg, Germany, a long-lasting feud across clans in the Aspromonte area in Calabria culminated in a bloody shoot-out (Sciarrone and Storti, 2014; Sergi and Lavorgna, 2016), leaving the city, and indeed Germany and Europe, shocked. Deputy Chief Constable 'G' of the Anti-Crime Central Directorate, highly knowledgeable on the 'ndrangheta, at the time stressed the resilience and capability of these clans, once considered less sophisticated and parochial. This ability has made it one of the most aggressive criminal groups in the world. From Calabria, where in the 1970s/80s the 'ndrangheta was active in the child-napping 'business' as a way of accumulating capital, the clans have developed to become leading drug traffickers and expanded beyond Calabria and Italian borders.[18]

As the 'ndrangheta will be the object of our case study, we will be analysing this mafia further in chapters 4 and 5. Having a heavy presence in the Italian northern regions and abroad, the 'ndrangheta clans' stronghold remains in Calabria, where mafia power is almost total and controls the territory in a capillary manner (Sciarrone in Serenata, 2014). Italian enforcement agencies agree on this analysis. Chief Constable 'R' of the Anti-Crime Central Directorate argues:

> Even if there are objective historical and socio-cultural differences among the three major Italian crime groups, the 'ndrangheta is the most able to be a power hub and exercises this power by making it very difficult for the police to be effective. The 'ndrangheta is less permeable to investigations, as having a family structure provides a shield against the phenomenon of the '*pentiti*' or 'justice collaborators' [whistle-blowers]. What makes 'ndrangheta clans stronger is the ability to blend within the social space that surrounds them. This capability has decreased in the Sicilian cosa nostra with time due to the efforts of the Italian judiciary and police forces.[19]

One of the recurrent points that representatives of the Italian law enforcement and judiciary – participants of our study – have pointed out is that unintentionally, the Calabrian 'social space' has favoured a resistance to any control or containment action against the 'ndrangheta. Often, family and group friendships and memberships in political parties, sport associations or secret societies – such as freemasonry – still exist and are powerful in the region, making it very difficult for investigators to determine where a mere individual's friendship with a specific 'ndrangheta member stops and where a mafia relationship begins.

Though historically, culturally and organisationally different, the mafias are essentially a social phenomenon – they are a power 'field' widely present in the Italian social space – in the south their presence is much denser, and in some territories appears to be totalising. As social sets of behaviours, they are bound to impact the surrounding social, cultural, economic and political domains.

Honourable societies? Mafia theories and practices

Italian and international analyses focused – at the least at the beginning – more on the Sicilian mafia or cosa nostra, probably because of the notoriety of the

American La Cosa Nostra (LCN) and various film and TV drama representations (Gazzotti, 2016) such as *The Godfather*, *Goodfellas*, *The Sopranos*, *Gomorrah* and the very popular (in Europe, particularly in Germany) Italian '80s drama fiction '*la Piovra*'.[20] These cinematic representations to different degrees are exposés on mafia, but in some cases they have also contributed to glamorise the lives of its affiliates, influencing everyday language and becoming very lucrative because of the topic's popularity among different audiences.

One of the first analyses on the Sicilian cosa nostra was conducted by controversial Sicilian sociologist Alfredo Niceforo, who combines two different explanations of the origin and causes of the criminal organisation, one historical and the other in line with Lombroso's atavistic positivist theory of crime (Cf. Guidi, 2016).

In his work, Niceforo (1898, reprinted in 2012) divides the Italian population into '*Ari*' and '*Mediterranei*'; the Arians (north of Italy) were more socially cohesive than the individualistic 'Mediterraneans'. Despite being Sicilian, Niceforo argued that the Mediterranean 'race' was inferior, prone to violence and criminal activity. Similarly, Italian politician Niceforo Pasquale Villari published a letter in the magazine *Perseveranda* in 1861, focusing his analysis on the camorra (Montuori, 2009) and for the first time attempting to explain the causes of its existence, listing poverty, alienation of the peasantry, incompetency of local politicians and, most importantly, diffused corruption.

As culture is a set of acquired, cognitive and symbolic elements of human existence, theoretical explanations must consider the importance of culture in explaining mafia and its codes and social interactions. Lupo (2011) explains how mafia cultural codes are linked to local traditional values and that historically, mafia members were seen as representatives of a broader Sicilian typology. Sicilians were described as suspicious of the state, individualistic and prone to vigilantism, refraining from assuming any responsibilities towards society, lacking a sense of citizenship. These views – which started with Villari – have been harshly criticised as an expression of the 'Southern question', according to which there is an essential criminogenic component in the cultures of the south (Moe, 1998, pp. 51–57). Nevertheless, cultural approaches have been fundamental to the understanding of the behavioural components of mafia as a social phenomenon.

Hess and Osers (1973) affirm that the mafia normative system originates from Sicily's historical domination by other countries and contempt against the colonisers, which, with time, has promoted a normative-cultural system manifesting in conflict between the bureaucratic apparatus and a cultural logic of resistance and violence. The mafia 'logic' becomes a way of acting, a way of life. Hess and Osers' (1973) analysis is still current, and despite the incongruences of their conclusions – that this way of life represents the Sicilian way of life – they have been one of the first to identify mafia as a *method* to commit crimes rather than just an organisational criminal structure.

The Italian legislation points out this trait. The Law Rognoni – La Torre (no. 646/1982) introduced for the first time the crime of 'mafia-type' unlawful association, which indeed punishes associations employing the mafia method to advance their businesses. The mafia method includes the power of intimidation and an entrenched code of silence (*omertà*) to reach financial gains; *omertà* derives not always from fear but also from consensus, kinship affiliations and tolerance to these organisations (Sergi, 2014). Intimidation and *omertà* also combine with social consensus, economic profits, political power and territorial supremacy, creating a pernicious system where power and enterprise 'syndicates' (Block, 1980) tend to coexist.

Contrary to cultural explanations, economic explanations of the mafia phenomenon point out how social actions are not influenced by culture but by a calculation of profit. The mafia system is identified as an economic organisation in the business of providing 'protection' (Gambetta, 1993) to fill the void left by a perceived non-existent or distant state, as the previously mentioned story of Dr Galati written by Dickie (2004) exemplifies. A clear example of this protection function is explained as follows by 'ndrangheta whistle-blower Francesco Oliviero. As the local council of the Cornaredo village (near the northern city of Milan) was unable to evict and shut down the local travellers' camp, and as the women of the camp were, allegedly, stealing from elderly residents, Oliviero's clan – after negotiation attempts – detonated a bomb on an empty caravan as a warning and aided with local residents. Oliviero argues: "this [action] is because we 'get on with people'. Social consensus is very useful later when it is the moment for political elections" (*Il Fatto Quotidiano* – online, 2017).

The mafias' investments in protection are, in fact, 'Faustian pacts'; they sell protection to profit and, most importantly, to nurture the myths of being honourable and 'to get on with people' (Gazzotti, 2016). Mafia members are not only pursuing the accumulation of economic capital but also cultural, symbolic and, ultimately, social capital, which allow the clans to oversee and control the territories where they operate and to maintain their power.

Cultural and economic elements, therefore, blend to create a comprehensive understanding of the mafia phenomenon (Paoli, 2003). In mafia contexts, different interests are expressed by a multitude of social actors (entrepreneurs, politicians and bureaucrats), converging and aligning through consensus and shared acceptance of certain codes of behaviour (Sergi and Lavorgna, 2016). In these contexts, corruption becomes the bridge between different societal levels and social phenomena.

But how can corruption diffuse so widely to the point that it becomes normalised and scandals become in the perception of the public 'nonscandals'? How do mafia codes and practices become in some circumstances almost accepted and subconsciously considered as inevitable? Pierre Bourdieu's micro–macro theory of society may go some way to answering these questions.

Corruption and mafia: a Bourdieuian analysis

In 2017, Don Ciotti – Catholic priest as well as founder and president of the Italian Association '*Libera. Associazioni, nomi e numeri contro le mafie*' – speaking to journalists during a public debate on mafia, argued that in Italy, corruption and mafia are two sides of the same coin.[21] Certainly, corruption is the bridge where mafia power meets the country's local and national power systems; this social milieu is bound to condition every social domain in the country, including the multibillion industry that is soccer.

The concepts of field, *doxa* (logic) and *habitus*, integral to Pierre Bourdieu's praxeology, may help in understanding these dynamics: how corruption meets mafia and then soccer; how corruption seems to permeate every domain of Italian social space, denoting a potential internalisation process;

how mafia power is – in specific geographical locations – considered an unofficial player in the local governance system and so integrated in the local social fabric that, as we indicated earlier in the chapter, it becomes very difficult to discriminate where the state action stops and the mafia begins.

Theory and practice: Bourdieu, *habitus* and field

French sociologist Pierre Bourdieu was fundamentally a structuralist, sharing the idea that the social space is populated by structures independent from the will and conscience of social actors constraining their practices; however, this control is not totalising – structures condition but do not necessarily determine human practices.

According to Bourdieu (1998), humans naively learn about the world and accept its axioms in a pre-reflective unconscious way, providing that it is in line with a pre-established mental *schema* (which Bourdieu terms *habitus*) and that it is primarily formed by past experiences. Social actors are also motivated in their practices by a constant unconscious/semi-conscious calculation of profit. This 'practical sense' is explained by Bourdieu:

> One of the privileges associated with the fact of being born in a game is that one can avoid cynicism since one has a feel for the game; like a good tennis player, one positions oneself not where the ball is but where it will be; one invests oneself and one invests not where the profit is, but where it will be.
>
> (Bourdieu, 1998, p. 79)

Practices are, therefore, the result of a situation and the unconscious mental schemata-*habitus*. Habitus is a

> system of durable and transposable dispositions which, integrating all past experiences, functions at every moment as a matrix of perceptions, appreciations, and actions, and makes it possible to accomplish infinitely differentiated tasks, thanks to the analogical transfer of schemata acquired in prior practice.
>
> (Bourdieu in Wacquant, 2016, p. 66)

Wacquant (2016) clarifies this concept, adding that *habitus* has an 'individuation' side: "Each person, by virtue of having a unique trajectory and location in the world, internalizes a matchless combination of such schemata" (p. 67). According to Bourdieu (1989), via *habitus*, social actors face the situations life throws at them; it is a mental filter which allows us to see – or not to see – options, and the occurrence or the reoccurrence of specific practices; "it implies a sense of one's place but also a sense of the place of others" (p. 19).[22]

Habitus, hence, can be compared to a satellite navigator system that helps individuals to navigate a social space – a geographical space made of different regions. These regions are what Bourdieu identified as 'fields',[23] relatively autonomous microcosms governed by specific logics – or *doxa* – and by forms of authority. Economy, religion, politics, education and, as we argue, mafia and soccer, are all fields. Each field is occupied by dominant individuals and groups belonging to the power field – which Bourdieu believed to have a great influence on the whole structure of the social space.

Fields have common traits; they are dominated by conflicts to control resources – what Bourdieu identified as 'capitals'. Each field has dominant and dominated actors, and each actor occupies a position established according to the quantity and structure of capital they possess (Bourdieu and Wacquant, 2007). So, while the *habitus* affects practices from the inside of the actor, the field affects the outside, offering social actors a range of positions and movements that the agent can or cannot adopt. It is the *habitus* that, as a mental filter, allows the actors to see or to disregard options and opportunities (Bourdieu and Wacquant, 2007). Field and *habitus* interrelate and work via capital and *doxa*.

Doxa differs from the law, which is publicly legitimised and presented as an obligation that every social actor must follow. Doxa is the product of a tacit agreement; it is "the universe of the undisputed [. . . what] goes without saying because it comes without saying" (Bourdieu, 1977, pp. 167–168); it represents what seems obvious, normal in that field, and consequently tends to influence the social space and social actors' perceptions.

Capitals, instead, determine the positions of social actors in the field. They can be economic (material and financial resources, or means of production), cultural (which includes languages, taste, way of life), symbolic (rituals, the external and internal recognition of symbols and values, such as mafia honour[24]), and finally social, which represents the totality of the actors' social relations: their social network (Bourdieu and Wacquant, 2007).

The social space made up of different fields is ultimately based on power. Bourdieu sees power culturally and symbolically created and constantly re-legitimised via relations between fields and *habitus*. However, as explained earlier, Bourdieu was an atypical structuralist, so *habitus* can be modified, and *doxa* can change. As Wacquant (2016) points out: "dispositions [which form the *habitus*] are socially mounted and can be eroded, countered or even dismantled by exposure to novel external forces, as demonstrated by situations of migration and specialized training" (p. 66). Despite the strong influence of the field, *habitus* can change when it does not fit the field or because the field's dynamics and *doxa* are changing, but this modification requires time (Bourdieu, 2009).

So how is *habitus* acquired, shaped, modified or reinforced? The primary *habitus* – acquired during youth-hood – tends to persist in time,[25] but some modifications can occur via a combination of different factors such as vicinity or distance from other actors and also 'mimeticism' in the field. Lizardo (2009) explains how mimeticism works, mentioning Wacquant: "While beginning as a process of consciously paying attention to visually available role models, during the course of training [Wacquant uses a pugilistic training example], this process of motor-schematic mirroring comes to acquire a habitual and tacit cast" (p. 720). Via mimeticism,[26] abstract principles and dispositions are passed on and these are used when similar situations and practices reoccur.

Social actors who inhabit the same field in the social world develop comparable *habitus* and a comprehension-led mechanism influenced by this mental filter (Simons and Burt, 2011); hence, they share similar hopes, choices and practices. Indeed, social actors/individuals can react differently to the same circumstances, because they may have had different social conditioning, or they become more conscious (reflexivity) and override their *habitus*. In essence, Bourdieu considers the unconscious as a key trait to understand the link between individual and social structures, and it may explain widely diffused, regular and predictable social practices such as corruption-related practices, the mafia method, tolerance and normalisation.

Corruption? Practice makes perfect

I live in the South – in Sicily – and I grew up in this region. Corruption is not only a problem infesting the South of the country but also in the North. The Tangentopoli (Bribesville) scandal uncovered to the judiciary in Milan a system of power led by corruption as its main logic.[27]

As the previous quote points out, corruption as a logic – *doxa* – and consequently corruption-related practices seem widely diffused in the whole country. However, in the southern regions, the links between the local power field, in many cases corruption led, and mafia power appear to be so severe that it seems in the eyes of Italians – especially those living in the southern regions – almost inevitable. In fact, in public perception, corruption appears to permeate daily life, spilling over in all social domains. In Italy, corrupt practices are variegated and sophisticated. For instance, peculiar to the Italian social, political and cultural milieu, the *raccomandazione* (recommendation), nepotism and clientelism are extremely diffused corruption-related practices.

La raccomandazione is the practice of being recommended by the 'right' person (often a politician or a high-ranking bureaucrat) for a job, even if the applicant might not be the best candidate – a practice which is clearly against the rules and laws of competition and transparency. *La raccomandazione* is widely used in many fields of the Italian social space, including soccer[28] and education. In soccer, the most famous example of *raccomandazione* is represented by the case of Al Saadi Gheddafi,[29] the son of Libyan dictator Muammar Gheddafi, who 'played' from 2003 to 2007 in Serie A for the Perugia FC, Udinese FC and Sampdoria FC, setting the unenviable record of having played twice during this timeframe and being disqualified in 2003 for doping.[30]

In higher education, as well, *la raccomandazione* meets nepotism and creates a situation where, essentially, becoming a full-time academic is often considered to be a right of birth. For instance, in 2016 in the city of

Bari (Southern Puglia region), it was found that 42 out of 176 economic lecturers were relatives of senior academics (*Il Corriere della Sera* – online, 2016). It doesn't occur only in Bari; *la raccomandazione* is very useful in gaining top marks in exams; in 2013 at the University of Perugia, some students allegedly received top marks because of the influence of a local politician (*la Repubblica* – online, 2013), who was then arrested for corruption[31] for the award of public contracts. In this context, it is not surprising that research carried out in 2015 by the University La Sapienza of Rome found that 43% of students who answered to the survey would willingly accept a recommendation to get the job of their dreams.[32]

Undoubtedly, *la raccomandazione* is a form of corrupt practice, even if there is no exchange of money or favours from the corruptor and the corrupt agent. Corradino (ANAC) is clear on this:

> This type of corrupt practice kills merit because it does not give the youngsters the possibility to showcase their abilities. One of the most important points here is 'transparency'; we have some data [ANAC] that shows that there is correlation between the Transparency International Index of corruption and the 'brain drain' phenomenon that currently appears to be hitting Italy hard. When I go to schools and speak to children about corruption, how it as a logic directly touches their lives, and that it does not give them the possibility to 'emerge' and push themselves, they show an (I believe healthy) anger in response. There is a survey done by Eurispes asking children when they feel their state is supporting them; the majority of respondents said yes, when it fights corruption, but they also replied that the state is not helpful when they do not find a job opportunity. I see the *raccomandazione* having dramatic effects because our country kills meritocracy.[33]

La raccomandazione and nepotism are effective means used by people in power to preserve their power. Italian journalist and writer Vittorio Gorresio claimed that Italy was a republic founded on the *raccomandazione* and that this national institution had the same origins of freemasonry, the Sicilian mafia and the Neapolitan camorra (*Il Fatto Quotidiano* – online, 2016). This widely diffused practice – especially in the southern part of the country – is an indicator of Jurist Henry Maine's differentiation between status and contract societies (Maine in Tönnies, 1988, pp. 192–193); in the first type of society statuses are ascribed; in the latter they are acquired, and twenty-first-century Italy seems still to belong to the former one.

In the southern part of the country, the *raccomandazione* often meets (political) clientelism – "the distribution of selective benefits to individuals or clearly defined groups in exchange for political support" (Hopkin, 2006, p. 1). Clientelism is expected when it is linked to mafia influences and pressures, as the case involving the arrest of Italian MP Antonio Caridi in 2016 seems to show. Caridi allegedly had a link with 'ndrangheta boss Girolamo Giovinazzo (Jimmy) of the Raso-Gullace-Albanese clan. The antimafia investigation accuses Caridi of gaining his elected MP status from votes provided by Jimmy. According to the investigators, Caridi allegedly influenced the recruitment of people linked to the 'ndrangheta in companies owned by both private investors and the state.[34]

Caridi's story is just one of the many 'scandals' reported almost daily by Italian media, showing how corruption has become integral part of the Italian power field at local and national levels. Italian philosopher Norberto Bobbio (1980)[35] describes the power field as invisible, where discretion and lack of accountability reign and corrupt practices become implicitly 'common sense knowledge'.

If we consider corruption as *doxa* – rules of the power game – we can see how this can be easily embedded in a *habitus* which may promote a view that 'things have always been that way' and cannot be changed. Corruption may also become for social actors both a way of making sense of others' practices and their own. Internalised in mental schemata-*habitus*, corruption as *doxa* also can influence choices and practices by facilitating the identification of accomplices and by marginalising those non-conformers to corrupt practices because they do not fit the fields' dynamics. This process has been supported by recent studies. Behavioural economists Gächter and Schulz (2016) point out that widely diffused corruption-related practices shape the moral action of citizens, implying that they contribute to a sense of inevitability and normalisation of corruption-related practices.

In 2016, Pope Francis, without researching, reached the same conclusion of Gächter and Schulz (2016) to explain this internalisation process into mental schemata, using a figure of speech comparing corruption to an '*abito mentale*' (mental cloak); corruption was described as a mind-set in Italy, common, recurrent and, most of all, ranging across different levels of seriousness (*La Repubblica* – online, 2016).

There are instances that support more widely the thesis of a process of internalisation of illicit practices. For example in 2016, during a corruption prevention initiative in a high school in the northern Italian city of Rimini, despite the fact that the students were quite keen to reject strong cases of corrupt behaviour, they seemed to condone those illicit practices that were close to their daily lives, for instance illegal downloading of films and music from the internet or not paying the fares for the bus and the tube (*Il Resto del Carlino* – online, 2016).

These findings may show an unconscious disposition to forgive minor episodes of illicit practices because more serious practices are happening anyway. Italian Judge PierCamillo Davigo (2017) provides a clear example of *habitus* at work in relation to corruption-led practices. Davigo writes about his experiences as public prosecutor, including those regarding a 27-year-old civil servant who admitted to the judiciary that he had received kickbacks in four instances. Davigo underlines that until that moment, he imagined 'the corrupt' to be different in some way from 'ordinary' people. He was surprised to see how 'normal' the offender was, saying: "he was like me; he could have been my university friend, a friend with whom I go dancing. . . ." He asked the offender: "How can a young man like you sell himself for just 250,000 Lire [approximatively €250]?" The offender was quiet and then replied: "You cannot understand because you belong to a world where these choices can be made individually; to be honest or dishonest depends on you. After the 15 days I was in the job, I saw that in that office everyone was corrupt! And I also understood that they would have not tolerated the presence of an honest man as a colleague. I would have lost my job – the 250,000 Lire was given to me by my line manager. I was on probation . . . I did not have the courage to refuse" (p. 22 Kindle edition).

In this example, *habitus* works as a 'horse blinder', unconsciously proposing only those options that fit the field's *doxa* and that can provide a sense of one's place and the place of others. Bourdieu uses the term 'interest' or later '*illusio*' to explain situations when individuals are "taken in by the game" (Bourdieu and Wacquant, 2007, p. 98) and commit to reproduce the *doxa* within the field without realising it.

This dynamic seems to be supported by the Italian social research firm, SWG, which reported in 2014 that half of the surveyed Italians attributed the responsibility for the increase in corrupt practices not only to politicians but also to fellow citizens (Termometropolitico, 2014). Two out of three participants agreed with the statement: "If they have a chance, Italians are corruptible." In 2007, only half of those surveyed had agreed with this statement.

If corruption seems to find a way to be internalised in the people's *habitus* or – to use the term of Pope Francis – is worryingly becoming a 'mental cloak', it seems fair to ask what happens when in certain parts of the country, like some areas of the south, corruption as a *doxa* of the local power field meets mafia power, its method, *doxa* and practices?

Mafia as another Italian 'power field'

"The real power [in Italy] is not the political one but the mafia."[36] This quote of the executive director of Transparency International-Italia could be accused of being overly pessimistic, but it seems to be matched by Italian social surveys and the perception of the Italians on this incredibly complex social phenomenon.[37]

Not only are Italians pessimistic about the diffusion of corruption, but they are also sceptical about the resolve of the state against the mafia clans. For instance, in 2016, the Centro Pio La Torre of Palermo (in Sicily) surveyed high school students – 39% believed that mafia was stronger than the Italian state and 20% believed that the only choice was to live with it (*Il Fatto Quotidiano* – online, 2016).

As explained earlier, a common misconception about mafia is that it operates only in the southern regions of the country, when, on the contrary: "The mafias, especially the 'ndrangheta, operate whenever there is a profit to be made."[38]

The mafias tend to control illegal markets, including – as chapters 4 and 5 will detail – those linked to soccer; this goes beyond the regions of Campania, Sicily and Calabria and beyond the Italian border as well. Calderoni (2012) provided a snapshot on where the mafias are active in Italy, and although it clearly shows that mafia clans are present in almost all of the Italian regions, at the same time it hints that the pervasiveness of mafia power in the south of Italy manifests differently. In other words, mafia presence and control of the territory – in the southern part of the country – seems to be all-encompassing. Thus, it should not be surprising that several instances of 'scandals' in soccer directly involving the mafias are often related to local soccer teams located in the south. It is also important to point out that criminal organisations such as cosa nostra, 'ndrangheta and camorra clans have in common the ability to maximise social capital to effectively achieve their licit and illicit purposes. They are very effective in creating bonds of trust with social actors (Gambetta, 1996).

Because of this *modus operandi*, mafia can be conceptualised as a power field which, at the local level in the southern regions, tends to superimpose onto the ordinary power field composed of local politicians, businessmen, bureaucrats, masonic lodges and even the Catholic church, as 'Operation Johnny' in 2017 demonstrates.[39] Italian Judge Rocco Chinnici clearly portrayed the mafia (in this case cosa nostra) as a power field; in one of his last interviews,[40] Chinnici argued for the first time that "Mafia is a method of doing politics by violence, hence it is crucial that mafia clans always look out for alliances, complicities with politics, hence with [the country's] power [system]."[41]

Corruption becomes in certain contexts even more of a stable bridge between the 'ordinary' power field and mafia power:

> Via its legal and illegal activities mafia aims to impose a capillary territorial control by becoming effectively 'the' power system. . . . It is also important to point out that the relationship among politics, public administration, business and mafia has changed; before there was a system where illicit money was divided mainly among these actors, so four interests must converge – if this did not occur, mafia clans would have employed violence; now all has changed, now mafia clans seem to have ditched violence and use corruption to reinforce their power.[42]

In Bourdieuian terms, mafia finds itself in the advantageous position to exercise symbolic violence.[43] Mafia power exercises symbolic violence by tacitly conditioning people, practices and social relationships at the same time, by offering to those who become part of this world symbolic capital opportunities (status and prestige), and a wide social network (social capital).

As a (power) field, mafia has its own *doxa* (logic) founded on 'myths' – traditional values (among them, honour, courage, justice, *omertà*), rituals and symbols that not only reinforce the belonging of individuals to these groupings, but also support a discourse that ennobles mafia clans in the eyes of the population while at the same time being used to shape mafia members' *habitus*, often displaying sacred/religious connotations.

The use of rituals and, often, religious symbols is, for example, strongly evident in the 'ndrangheta's 'method' and its misappropriation of the Archangel Michael as the patron saint of some clans,[44] as the Vatican Church magazine *Famiglia Cristiana* has pointed out several times (*Famiglia Cristiana* – online, 2015). The Archangel Michael represents justice, and for this reason he is also – ironically – the patron saint of the Italian police. The not-so-subtle message here is to symbolically justify 'ndrangheta actions as 'just' and equal, even though the clans clearly oppose the official justice system.

Mafia *doxa* may not be internalised only by its members – this process finds its way into the *habitus* of those who share the same social space where the clans 'rule'. Italian Calabrian-born journalist and Libera (Italian antimafia association) expert Bruno Palermo explains how the mafia clans' *doxa* and *habitus* are difficult to challenge. Palermo challenges the myth that 'ndrangheta and mafia do not harm children, because they are 'honourable'. Palermo argued:

> In my book [Palermo, 2016] I tell the stories of 108 children killed by the mafias in Italy; we [Calabrians] for instance grew up listening to these tales that the 'ndrangheta has an honour code that defends people from the state or help because the state is not visible in our region. A 10-year-old child who was playing soccer with other children was caught in a shoot-out and cross-fire between the 'soldiers'

of two rival clans. When this tragedy occurred, the father heard from 'people' that the child was unlucky and at the wrong place at the wrong time. This almost unconscious explanation seems to justify the assassins and safeguard this cloak of honour always proudly displayed by mafia criminals. But how is it possible that a soccer pitch is the wrong place for a 10-year-old child? In a 'normal' society where people do the right thing, a soccer pitch is not the wrong place for a child; there is no wrong place for an innocent; the wrong place is for the killers, for the mafiosi in our society.[45]

Without generalising, it is evident that what Palermo affirms is plausible when the social spaces of specific regions such as Calabria are analysed. On several occasions, Nicola Gratteri, the chief public prosecutor of Catanzaro – executive capital of the Calabria region – and world expert on the 'ndrangheta has affirmed that the 'ndrangheta has progressively become the leader of the country and stated, "The 'ndrangheta, but also camorra and [Sicilian] mafia have become an integral part of society because they are able somewhat to obtain trust from citizens with low morals and/or economic problems."[46]

Gratteri's economic justification is not reductive. Barbagallo (2011) underlines, for instance, the long-unresolved issue of Italy's north-south divide,[47] which is more striking considering that, as already stated, Italy is a member of the G7 and the eighth-largest world economy.[48]

Within this social space, social practices arise from such structural (structured and structuring) experiences which already have, as their defining principle, the expression of a certain way of perceiving the world according to a particular *doxa* with specific interests. Di Blasi et al. (2014) show that the process of internalisation of mafia *doxa* may occur in relation to youth development – the period which structures the primary *habitus* – in territories where mafia power is totalising. Di Blasi et al.'s (2014) study focused on the youth of three regions (Calabria, Campania and Sicilia) and found evidence of a process of internalisation of mafia *doxa*, the most important of which is *omertà* (silence for mafia protection).[49] In Sicily, for instance, the researchers pointed out that, from childhood, the participants learned that in their daily lives there were events that they were allowed to speak about and others that they should pretend not to know; if they spoke in the family about mafia, they were answered that the less they knew, the better it would be for them. Mafia was a heavy burden that entangled with their lives, leaving them with the dilemma to accept this status quo or to try to change it. In Naples, the findings of Di Blasi et al. (2014) were particularly interesting, as it seems *omertà* was combined with the crucial need to know as in depth as possible about the camorra *doxa* in order to improve one's chances of survival. As the researchers argue, in Scampia – a neighbourhood where the clans' presence is very strong – the more the youth knew about the camorra clans' *doxa*, the more they felt able to defend themselves. So they learned for instance to avoid being identified as undercover police officers, to recognise the 'sentinels' at the entrance of a camorra-controlled district as well as the sound of little bells from the roofs signalling that the police were arriving. They learned consciously about the camorra while seemingly unconsciously adapting their praxis to fit those of the clans. These research findings seem to fit well with what Bourdieu (2009) terms as unconscious calculation of profits due to necessity.

It is, however, in the Italian Calabria region that this *habitus*-shaping process seems even more prominent, as Di Blasi et al.'s (2014) study shows; in this region, mafia power and the 'ordinary' local power field are almost perfectly superimposed. The distinction between the two fields of power has become blurred; Calabria is the number one Italian region for mafia infiltrations in the local economic milieu (*La Repubblica* – online, 2016); in November 2017, five municipality councils – including the large town of Lamezia Terme, were dissolved by the Italian government for 'ndrangheta collusions'[50] – collusions which are also significant to make sense of the Calabrian soccer 'style', as chapter 5 will highlight.

Entering the pitch: Italy vs corruption and mafia

Even though corruption and mafia are historic problems in Italy, it would be biased not to mention the sacrifice in terms of resources, but also lives, of the Italian judiciary and security agencies that have tried – at times without enough support from the political classes – to ensure that no Italian territory became a no-go zone in the hands of mafia clans, while at the same time 'cleaning' the political, bureaucratic and economic sectors of corruption-related practices.

In 2012, Law no. 190[51] (November 6) included "dispositions for the prevention and repression of corruption in public administration". Despite the good intentions, it was immediately evident that Law 190 focused only on public administrators, without including political power, which more often is at the core of corruption 'scandals'. Law no. 190 increases the minimum imprisonment tariff for misappropriation of public funds, punishing corrupt acts committed by private citizens and/or illicit forms of lobbyism; the sanction is imprisonment for two to three years. However, the most important measure was to institute the 'Autorità Nazionale Anticorruzione – ANAC' (The Italian Anti-Corruption Authority), which approves a national anti-corruption strategy written by the Department of Public Service, and analyses the causes of corruption to devise intervention and prevention strategies.

We asked Michele Corradino[52] if ANAC was an effective tool against corruption:

> I believe that ANAC is useful to make life difficult for the corrupted, corrupters and dodgy dealmakers; we have in Italy a judiciary that does a superb job in a very difficult socio-economic context. However, Italy has a system of statutes of limitation in criminal procedure that make it very difficult for the prosecutors to convict offenders [they have a relatively short time to convict offenders]. As the corrupted and corrupters have the interest to keep their criminal pact secret, investigations are long and only likely to uncover corruption-related practices when there is a whistle-blower or there are wiretappings to speed up the process. It is also important to remember that when the judiciary and the police act, the crime has been already committed; thus, we need prevention more than repression.[53]

ANAC, with all its limitations, has been a powerful tool in tackling systemic corruption and its link to the mafias, but to date not powerful enough. As

Corradino argues, the certainty and severity of punishment must be fully implemented to work as a deterrent, and it is important to issue a 'red card' to the corrupted by removing them permanently from the power field. As far as the Italian state action against the mafias is concerned, Italy's antimafia legislation is one of the most advanced legislations against organised crime in the West, and the professionalism of the Italian antimafia agencies is highly regarded worldwide.

It is important to stress that the fight against the mafia continues incessantly by the Italian judiciary and police forces with important results, namely arrests and convictions of mafia clan members, capture of fugitives and seizures of mafia clan assets. This has been possible because of *ad hoc* organisational and investigative tools and because of very sophisticated antimafia legislation, especially in terms of confiscation of financial assets and of normative tools and consolidated practices carried out in collaboration with the international security forces community. This state political, judicial and investigative resolve originated in the 1990s because of the terrorist strategy carried out by the Sicilian Cosa Nostra, and it is founded on the ideas and analyses of judges Giovanni Falcone (assassinated with his wife Francesca Morvillo in May 1992) and Paolo Borsellino (in July 1992), both killed together with their protection officers in Palermo. Since then, the answer of the Italian state has shifted from a reactive-emergency response to a structural and more effective strategy based on the effective sharing of intelligence between the Direzione Investigativa Antimafia (Antimafia Investigation Directorate – DIA), the Italian police forces and the Direzione Nazionale Antimafia e Antiterrorismo (antimafia and antiterrorism national directorate – a judiciary unit which enforces the Italian antimafia laws and, more recently, antiterrorism laws).[54]

Specifically, the DIA is an *ad hoc* antimafia intelligence and security force which was established in 1991 and is part of the Public Security Department of the Italian Ministry of the Interior, composed of highly trained personnel of the Italian State Police, the Carabinieri (military force with police functions), the Guardia di Finanza (Italian financial police) and the Polizia Penintenziaria (Penitentiary Police).[55]

The Italian antimafia legal arsenal instead pivots around the definition of mafia-type unlawful association (article 416-bis of the Italian criminal code), which defines the sociological traits of the mafia method and seeks to standardise juridical responses to it. The antimafia system, however, includes both direct and indirect measures to fight this phenomenon, ranging from criminal law to administrative procedures (like the dissolution of town councils for mafia infiltration), all the way to family law provisions and obviously economic norms on confiscation and money laundering (Sergi, 2014). Even though the links between legislations on corruption and antimafia legislations are obvious and investigations often overlap, anti-corruption has been given a new face in Italy in recent years.

In 2013, the Italian government led by former Prime Minister Enrico Letta instituted a task force to fight the mafias,[56] which underlined the need to promote urban (by improving public spaces and housing conditions) and educational (by promoting resistance to logics of usurpation and personal gain against the common good) changes, while improving the job market to stop mafia clans from imposing social control via the offer of jobs through their own personal connections.

Within the 'social space' analysed in this chapter, Italian soccer and its links to mafia should become more evident. Mafia power intertwines with Italian soccer's economic, structural, social and, most importantly, ethical weaknesses in the same fashion as it does with the country's power system and all its vulnerabilities. In Italian soccer, the mafia identifies exceptional economic but also equally important symbolic and social capital potentials; this *modus operandi* is extremely efficient as well as easy to follow considering that corruption has been part of professional Italian soccer since 1922, as the next chapter will point out.

Notes

1 Tangentopoli is a scandal that affected Italy in the '90s. It is a system of corruption and illicit financing that involved the leaders of Italy's power field. It also marked the disappearance of two major political parties – la Democrazia Cristiana (The Christian Democrats) and il Partito Socialista Italiano-The Italian Socialist Party (Cf. Barbacetto et al., 2012).
2 Cf. www.admin.ch/gov/en/start/dokumentation/medienmitteilungen.msg-id-58891.html
3 Cf. www.theguardian.com/football/2015/may/27/several-top-fifa-officials-arrested

4 www.rainews.it/dl/rainews/articoli/Scandalo-Mose-Venezia-sotto-choc-arrestato-il-sindaco-Orsoni-b52189cf-ae92-4677-a57d-19f104f5e34f.html
5 Controversial Russian adviser of the Romanov of Russian Tsar Nicholas II. Cf. www.agi.it/cronaca/2016/12/16/news/raffaele_marra_arrestato_ecco_spiegata_la_vicenda-1317055/
6 Cf. https://research.vu.nl/ws/portalfiles/portal/2286233
7 Ibid.
8 Ibid.
9 Cf. p. 78 at http://library.la84.org/SportsLibrary/SoccerStudies/1999/FS0202h.pdf
10 Excerpt 3 interview DM (2017).
11 Cf. www.repubblica.it/cronaca/2016/07/19/news/_ndrangheta_quaranta_arresti_in_tutta_italia_contro_cosche_reggine-144409232/
12 The famous expression 'cosa nostra' (our thing) indicates a criminal organisation that is peculiar, regrettably, to Italy, namely the Sicilian mafia. The term is not actually Italian in origin but derives from the American conceptualisation of Italian organised crime in the 1950s/60s following the testimonies of justice witness Joe Valachi (Cf. Paoli in Albanese, 2014).
13 Excerpt 3 interview R (2017).
14 'There Will Be Blood – the Unmissable, Ultimate Mafia Show Gomorrah Is Back'; cf. www.theguardian.com/tv-and-radio/2016/may/11/gomorrah-returns-second-series-unmissable-mafia-crime-show-robert-saviano
15 'Nicola Cosentino condannato a 7 anni e 6 mesi. Condannati anche i fratelli'; cf. www.ilsole24ore.com/art/notizie/2017-03-15/nicola-cosentino-condannato-7-anni-e-6-mesi-condannati-anche-fratelli-210555.shtml?uuid=AEcoIQn
16 Cf. www.ecodibergamo.it/stories/Cronaca/il-boss-della-camorra-pentitoi-nostri-rifiuti-sepolti-al-nord_1212061_11/
17 Cf. Ciconte mentioned by Parini, http://scienzepolitiche.unical.it/bacheca/archivio/materiale/1452/Parini-voce%27ndrangheta.pdf
18 Excerpt 12 interview G (2017).
19 Excerpt 6a interview R (2017).
20 In Italian, *Piovra* means the Octopus; the term figuratively refers to the Sicilian cosa nostra's many tentacles on the country political, economic and social domains.
21 'Mafia Roma: Ciotti, con corruzione faccia stessa medaglia'; cf www.ansa.it/legalita/rubriche/cronaca/2015/06/13/mafia-roma-ciotticon-corruzione-faccia-stessa-medaglia_62cd3f07-fc1c-49be-b87c-0b3cf23c20a2.html
22 Habitus can be described as the unconscious part of the mind. Bourdieu's focus on the unconscious to understand human practices is supported by recent neuroscience studies; unconscious system processes seem to be the silent engine of human psychological functions (Ginot, 2015; Bargh, 2014; Damasio, 2010; Glaser and Kihlstrom, 2007; Koziol and Budding, 2010).

Ginot (2015) argues that the "unconscious is in essence an instrumental system that actively relates to the external world and learns through perceptions, priming, and actions" (Ginot, 2015, p. 34).

23 A field is "a network or configuration of objective relations between positions occupied by social actors" (Bourdieu and Wacquant, 2007, p. 97); in fields, actors manifest and reproduce dispositions (*habitus*).

24 John Peristiany (1965) was one of the first sociologists to focus on the concept of 'honour' and 'shame' as fundamental values of Mediterranean societies. Honour has traditionally been at the top of social values, influencing the society's hierarchical order as it divides members in two groups: those who are honourable and those who are deprived of honour. However, as Ergaver (2015) points out, honour is difficult to maintain and must be constantly proved and asserted. This dynamic uncovers a psychological blackmail process; to maintain honour and being valued and respected, an individual must abide by what the society or community considers as acceptable norms. If this is not done, the individual is shamed and cast out. Honour, shame, ritual and myth are recurring concepts used as means to internalise the mafia *doxa* and to promote conformism.

25 Cf. Grenfell (2008).

26 The Greek philosopher Aristotle was the first to explain this dynamic of learning by practice; in one of his most known quotes, he argued "For the things we have to learn before we can do them, we learn by doing them" (Aristotle translated by Ross, 1999, p. 21).

27 Michele Corradino a leading member of the Italian Autorita' Nazionale Anti Corruzione-ANAC; Excerpt 5a interview C (2017).

28 Cf. chapter 3 for more examples.

29 For many years the Libyan 'government' had strong economic ties with Italy; in 2014, the newspaper *Il Tempo* (*Il Tempo* – online, 2014) reported that 2 billion Euro were invested in Italy, including market shares of the Juventus FC.

30 'Doping, per Kallon e Gheddafi otto e tre mesi di squalifica'; cf. www. repubblica.it/2003/j/sezioni/sport/calcio/doping/ghedda/ghedda.html

31 'Indagine Tav a Firenze, arrestata l'ex presidente dell'Umbria Maria Rita Lorenzetti'; cf. www.perugiatoday.it/cronaca/indagine-tav-arresto-lorenzetti-16-settembre-2013.html

32 'Raccomandazione? Si, Grazie. L'indagine De La Sapienza Di Roma Per #Non CiFermaNessuno'; cf. www.napolitime.it/70977-raccomandazione-si-grazie-lindagine-dela-sapienza-di-roma-per-noncifermanessuno.html

33 Excerpt 9 interview C (2017).

34 'Voti della 'ndrangheta e assunzioni manovrate: il ruolo del senatore Caridi', cf. www.newsandcom.it/voti-della-ndrangheta-e-assunzioni-manovrate-il-ruolo-delsenatore-caridi-audio/

35 Cf. Vannucci, www.libertaegiustizia.it/2010/10/15/il-potere-invisibile-l%E2%80%99evoluzione-della-corruzione/
36 Executive Director of Transparency International-Italia; Excerpt 3 interview DM (2017).
37 Cf. The recent Demos (Italian social research agency) social survey titled 'Gli Italiani e la Mafia' (The Italians and the Mafia) carried out in December 2017, www.demos.it/a01467.php
38 Deputy Chief Constable 'G' Italian police, Excerpt 7 interview G (2017).
39 Cf. chapter 1.
40 In the same year, Chinnici was killed, along with two *carabinieri* (military police), by a car bomb.
41 'Intervista al Giudice Rocco Chinnici'; cf. www.antimafiaduemila.com/home/di-latua/237-vedi/50761-intervista-al-giudice-rocco-chinnici.html
42 Corradino (ANAC); Excerpt 14 interview C (2017).
43 According to Bourdieu (1999): "Symbolic violence is violence wielded with tacit complicity between victims and its agents, insofar as both remain unconscious" (p. 17).
44 Cf. Ciconte (2015).
45 Excerpt 15 interview BP (2017).
46 'Sconfiggere la mafia in 5 anni, ecco il piano di Nicola Gratteri'; cf. www.cosapubblica.it/sconfiggere-mafia-piano-nicola-gratteri/3320/
47 The north-south divide has extremely deep social and historical roots, as mentioned earlier in this book, converging with what is known as the Southern Question.
48 Ibid.
49 Cf. http://in-formality.com/wiki/index.php?title=Omert%E0
50 'Calabria, Cdm scioglie cinque comuni per mafia: c'è anche Lamezia'; cf. www.repubblica.it/politica/2017/11/22/news/calabria_cdm_comuni_sciolti_mafia_lamezia-181838338/
51 Cf. www.gazzettaufficiale.it/eli/id/2012/11/13/012G0213/sg
52 Michele Corradino is a leading member of the Italian Autorita' Nazionale Anticorruzione – ANAC.
53 Excerpt 20 interview C (2017).
54 La Direzione Nazionale Antimafia is an *ad hoc* judiciary unit which enforces the Italian antimafia law; it was established in 1992 and since 2015 also has had jurisdiction over terrorism (DNAA). The DNNA composes the National Antimafia Prosecutor and 20 public prosecutors. The national antimafia prosecutor exercises the functions of coordinating the investigations conducted by the district DNAA units (located throughout the country) on crimes committed by organised crime. The National Antimafia Prosecutor also has the power to coordinate the Italian central police services: the aforementioned

Antimafia Investigation Directorate (DIA), the elite unit of the Carabinieri (ROS), the Central Police Operation Service (SCO), and the Central Intelligence and Investigation service of the Guardia di Finanza (SCICO). Cf. www.giustizia.it/giustizia/it/mg_2_10_1.page

55 Cf. http://direzioneinvestigativaantimafia.interno.gov.it

56 'Letta, task force per lotta criminalità'; cf. www.lagazzettadelmezzogiorno.it/news/italia/468436/letta-task-force-per-lotta-criminalita.html

References

Allum, F., 2016. *The Invisible Camorra*. New York: Cornell University Press.
Aristotle, 1999. *Nichomachean Ethics*. Waterloo: Kitchener.
Barbacetto, G., Gomez, P. and Travaglio, M., 2012. *Mani Pulite, 25 anni dopo*. Milano: Chiarelettere.
Barbagallo, F., 2011. *Storia della Camorra*. Milano: Economica Laterza.
Bargh, J.A., 2014. Unconscious Impulses and Desires Impel What We Think and Do in Ways Freud Never Dreamed of. *Scientific American*, 310, pp. 30–38.
Block, A., 1980. *East Side–West Side: Organizing Crime in NewYork 1930–1950*. Cardiff: University College Cardiff Press.
Bobbio, N., 1980. La Democrazia e il potere invisibile. *Rivista Italiana di Scienza Politica*, 10, pp. 181–203.
Bourdieu, P., 2009. *Sociology in Question*. London: Sage.
Bourdieu, P., 1999. *On Television*. New York: New Press.
Bourdieu, P., 1998. *Practical Reason: On the Theory of Action*. Stanford: Stanford University Press.
Bourdieu, P., 1989. Social Space and Symbolic Power. *Sociological Theory*, 7(1), pp. 14–25.
Bourdieu, P., 1977. *Outline of a Theory of Practice*. Cambridge: Cambridge University Press.
Bourdieu, P. and Wacquant, L., 2007. *An Invitation to Reflexive Sociology*. Cambridge: Polity Press.
Brooks, R., 1909. The Nature of Political Corruption. *Political Science Quarterly*, 24(1), pp. 1–22.
Bruno, P., 2016. *Al Posto Sbagliato. Storie Di Bambini Vittime Di Mafia*. Cosenza: Rubbettino.
Calderoni, F., 2012. Although There Is Little Truth behind the "Godfather" Stereotype, Mafia Infiltration Remains a Serious Problem in Italian Politics. Available: http://eprints.lse.ac.uk/49557/ [November 4, 2016].
Carson, L., 2014-last update, Corruption: Beyond Rational Choice Theory [Homepage of SSRN], [Online]. Available: http://dx.doi.org/10.2139/ssrn.2520280 [June 4, 2016].

Ciconte, E., 2015. *Riti criminali. I codici di affiliazione alla 'ndrangheta.* Cosenza: Rubbettino.

Ciconte, E., 2011. *'Ndrangheta.* Soveria Mannelli, CZ: Rubbettino.

Coleman, J.W., 1987. Toward an Integrated Theory of White-Collar Crime. *The American Journal of Sociology*, 93(2), pp. 406–439.

Dalla Chiesa, N., 2012. *L'impresa mafiosa. tra capitalismo violento e controllo sociale.* Milano: Cavallotti University Press.

Damasio, A., 2010. *Self Comes to Mind: Constructing the Conscious Brain.* New York: Vintage Press.

Davigo, P., 2017. *Il sistema della corruzione.* Milano: Laterza.

Di Bella, S., 1991. *Risorgimento e Mafia in Sicilia: I mafiusi dell Vicaria di Palermo.* Cosenza: Luigi Pellegrini Editore.

Di Blasi, M., Cavani, P., La Grutta, S., et al., 2014. Crescere in terre di mafia. *Narrare i gruppi. etnografia dell'interazione quotidiana. Prospettive cliniche e sociali*, 9, pp. 55–70.

Dickie, J., 2004. *Cosa Nostra: A History of the Sicilian Mafia.* London: Hodder Paperbacks.

Di Nicola, A. and Zanella, M., 2011. Criminological Theories and Corruption: An Explanatory Study at the International Level. *Rassegna Italiana di Criminologia*, 2, pp. 37–44.

Ergaver, A., 2015. Mediterranean Values: The Honour and the Shame of Hospitality. *European Studies*, 1(2), pp. 111–123.

Eriksen, T.H., 2015. *Small Places, Large Issues: An Introduction to Social and Cultural Anthropology.* 4th edn. London: Pluto Press.

Famiglia Cristiana, 2015-last update, San Michele, Patrono Della Polizia Usurpato Dalla 'Ndrangheta. Available: www.famigliacristiana.it/articolo/san-michele-arcangelo-il-patrono-dellapolizia-tirato-per-le-ali-dalla-criminalita_590601.aspx [November 4, 2016].

Gächter, S. and Schulz, J.F., 2016. Intrinsic Honesty and the Prevalence of Rule Violations across Societies. *Nature*, 531(7595), pp. 496–499.

Gambetta, D., 1993. *The Sicilian Mafia: The Business of Private Protection.* Cambridge: Harvard University Press.

Gazzotti, E., 2016. *Teorie e direzioni progettuali di resistenza alle mafie.* Bologna: Alma Mater Studiorum – Università di Bologna.

Gibilaro, I. and Marcucci, C., 2005. *La criminalita' organizzata di stampo mafioso.* Ostia, Roma: Gaurdia di Finanza; Scuola di Polizia Tributaria.

Ginot, E., 2015. *The Neuropsychology of the Unconscious Integrating Brain and Mind in Psychotherapy.* New York: W.W. Norton & Company.

Glaser, J. and Kihlstrom, F., 2007. Compensatory Automaticity: Unconscious Volition Is Not an Oxymoron. In: Hassin, R., Uleman, J. and Bargh, J. (eds.). *The New Unconscious.* New York: Oxford University Press, pp. 171–196.

Gratteri, N., Maddalon, M., Nicaso, A. and Trumper, J., 2014. *Male lingue.Vecchi e nuovi codici delle mafie*. Cosenza: Pellegrini Editore.

Grenfell, M., ed., 2008. *Pierre Bourdieu: Key Concepts*. London: Routledge.

Guidi, F., 2016. *Cesare Lombroso e le razze criminali. Sulla teoria dell' inferiorita' die meridionali*. Lucca: Tra le righe libri.

Hess, H., 1998. *Mafia and Mafiosi: Origin, Power, and Myth*. NewYork: NewYork University Press.

Hess, H. and Osers, E., 1973. *Mafia and Mafiosi: The Structure of Power*. London: Ashgate Publishing Limited.

Hollway, W. (2006). *The Capacity to Care: Gender and Ethical Subjectivity*. London: Routledge.

Hopkin, J., 2006. Conceptualizing Political Clientelism: Political Exchange and Democratic Theory. *Concept Analysis: Unpacking Clientelism, Governance and Neoliberalism*, 31/08/2006, American Political Science Association, pp. 1–19.

Il Corriere della Sera-online, 2016-last update, Favori agli amici e concorsi truccati. In cattedra finiscono i figli dei prof. Available: www.corriere.it/cronache/16_settembre_24/favori-amici-concorsi-truccati-universita-professori-6ad74316-81cd-11e6-bb54-ccc86a7805dc.shtml [September 26, 2016].

Il Fatto Quotidiano-online, 2017-last update, Processo Aemilia, il boss della 'ndrina di Rho: "Con i kalashnikov e la dinamite abbiamo cacciato gli zingari". Available: www.ilfattoquotidiano.it/2017/03/22/processo-aemilia-il-boss-della-ndrina-di-rho-coni-kalashnikov-e-la-dinamite-abbiamo-cacciato-gli-zingari/3460349/ [June 20, 2017].

Il Fatto Quotidiano-online, 2016-last update, Mafia, il sondaggio tra gli studenti. Per il 39 percento "è più forte dello Stato". Available: www.ilfattoquotidiano.it/2016/01/29/mafia-il-sondaggio-tra-gli-studenti-per-il-39-percento-e-piu-forte-dello-stato/2418526/ [February 12, 2016].

Il Resto del Carlino-online, 2016-last update, Studenti contro politici e mafiosi. E assolvono i 'furbetti' del web. Available: www.ilrestodelcarlino.it/rimini/cronaca/corruzione-illegalita-voti-studenti-1.1697986 [September 5, 2017].

IlTempo-online, 2014-last update, Gaddafi's treasure embarrasses Rome. Available: www.iltempo.it/cronache/2014/11/21/news/il-tesoro-di-gheddafi-imbarazzaroma-960681/ [October 12, 2017].

Jansics, D., 2014. Interdisciplinary Perspectives on Corruption. *Sociology Compass*, pp. 358–372.

Koziol, L.F. and Budding, D.E., 2010. *Subcortical Structures and Cognition: Implications for Neuropsychological Assessment*. NewYork: Springer.

La Repubblica-online, 2016-last update, Il Papa scrive: "Corruzione, peccato che diventa un modo di vivere". Available: www.repubblica.it/vaticano/2016/01/10/news/un_brano_del_libro_di_francesco_corruzione_peccato_che_diventa_un_modo_di_vivere_-130936247/ [June 20, 2017].

La Repubblica-online, 2013-last update, Lorenzetti: "Quello studente va promosso" e il raccomandato prese 30 in patologia. Available: www.repubblica.it/cronaca/2013/09/24/news/lorenzetti_studente_raccomandato-67140682/ [September 07, 2017].

Lizardo, O., 2009. Is a "Special Psychology" of Practice Possible? From Values and Attitudes to Embodied Dispositions. *Theory & Psychology*, 19(6), pp. 713–727.

Lupo, S., 2011. *History of the Mafia*. New York: Columbia University Press.

Malinowski, B., 1926[2015]. *Myth in Primitive Psychology*. London: Kegan Paul, Trench, Trubner & Co.

Marquette, H. and Peiffer, C., 2015. Collective Action and Systemic Corruption. Available: https://ecpr.eu/Filestore/PaperProposal/b5944a31-85b6-4547-82b3-0d4a74910b07.pdf [September 12, 2016].

Martone, V., 2014. State, Markets, and Mafias: Political-Criminal Networks and Local Governance in the Campania Region. *The European Review of Organised Crime*, 1(2), pp. 57–80.

Moe, N., 1998. The Emergence of the Southern Question in Villari, Franchetti and Sonnino. In: Schneider, J. (ed.). *Italy's Southern Question: Orientalism in One Country*. New York and Oxford: Berg, pp. 51–77.

Montuori, F., 2009. *Lessico e Camorra. Storia della parola, proposte etimologiche e termini del gergo ottocentesco*. Napoli: Fridericiana Editrice Universitaria.

Natella, P., 2002. *La parola Mafia*. Firenze: Olschki Ed.

Niceforo, A., reprinted 2012. *L'Italia Barbara Contemporanea*. Firenze: Nabu Press.

Paoli, L., 2003. *Mafia Brotherhoods: Organized Crime, Italian Style*. Oxford: Oxford University Press.

Paoli, L., 2014. *Oxford Handbook of Organized Crime*. Oxford: Oxford University Press.

Peristiany, J.G., 1965. *Honour and Shame: The Values of Mediterranean Society*. London: Weidenfeld and Nicolson.

Sales, I., 1993. *La Camorra le Camorre*. Roma: Editori Riuniti.

Saviano, R., 2011. *Gomorra:Viaggio nell' impero economico e nel sogno di dominio della camorra*. Milano: Arnoldo Mondadori.

Scalia, V., 2016. *Crime Networks and Power: The Transformation of Sicilian Cosa Nostra*. London: Palgrave Macmillan.

Sciarrone, R., 2014. 'Ndrangheta: A Reticular Organization. In: Serenata, S. (ed.). *The 'Ndrangheta and Sacra Corona Unita: The History, Organization and Operations of Two Unknown Mafia Groups*. Berlin: Springer, pp. 81–99.

Sciarrone, R. and Storti, L., 2014. The Territorial Expansion of Mafia-Type Organized Crime: The Case of the Italian Mafia in Germany. *Crime, Law and Social Change*, 61(1), pp. 37–60.

Sergi, A., 2014. Organised Crime and the Law: Conspiracy and Membership Offences in Italian, English and International Frameworks. *King's Law Journal*, 25(2), pp. 185–200.

Sergi, A., and Lavorgna, A., 2016. 'Ndrangheta. The Glocal Dimensions of the Most Powerful Italian Mafia. London: Palgrave.

Simons, R. and Burt, C., 2011. Learning to Be Bad: Adverse Social Conditions, Social Schemas, and Crime. *Criminology*, 49(2), pp. 553–598.

The Telegraph-online, 2016-last update, Explained: David Cameron's Global Anti-Corruption Summit. Available: www.telegraph.co.uk/news/2016/05/12/explained-david-camerons-global-anti-corruption-summit/ [June 6, 2016].

Termometropolitico, 2014-last update, Sondaggio SWG su corruzione. Available: www.termometropolitico.it/1178293_sondaggio-swg-secondo-gli-italiani-politici-la-categoria-piu-corrotta-ma-imprenditori-e-cittadini-condividono-la-responsabilita-1406.html [November 8, 2016].

Tönnies, F., 1988. *Community and Society*. Hoboken, NJ: Transaction Publishers.

UK Department for International Development, 2015. Why Corruption Matters: Understanding Causes, Effects and How to Address Them. Available: www.gov.uk/government/uploads/system/uploads/attachment_data/file/406346/corruption-evidence-paper-why-corruption-matters.pdf [October 15, 2016].

Vannucci, A., 2010. *L' evoluzione della corruzione in Italia: evidenza empirica, fattori facilitanti, politiche di contrasto*. Available: www.astrid-online.it/static/upload/protected/Vann/Vannucci.pdf

Varese, F., 2011. *Mafias on the Move*. New York: Princeton University Press.

Wacquant, L., 2016. A Concise Genealogy and Anatomy of Habitus. *The Sociological Review*, 64(1), pp. 64–72.

Chapter 3

Scandals, the 'sins' and 'sinners' of Italian soccer

In July 2017,[1] the public prosecutors of the city of Prato, Tuscany, arranged for the arrest of the president of the Sestese Soccer Club – a team playing in the Italian amateur division 'Eccellenza Toscana'. The alleged offences were illegal immigration of African minors to be employed in various Italian soccer teams under false documentation and match-fixing involving 11 matches of the lower divisions of Lega Pro, Eccellenza Toscana and the Tuscan Regional Promotion Championship. Among with what soccer fans would classify as 'dodgy' matches, there was also the notorious – for the cities and fans' historical rivalry – Chiusi vs Sestese fixture, played in Chiusi on May 7, 2017 which, according to fans, was negatively influenced by 'scandalous' unilateral decisions by the referee in favour of the Sestese FC.

In the same month, another 'scandal' hit media scrutiny, this time in Spain. The president of the Real Federación Española de Fútbol (the Spanish soccer federation), Angel Maria Villar, was arrested for corruption on suspicion of embezzling funds (*The Guardian* – online, 2017). Even though the Spanish soccer corruption scandal reminds fans that corruption in soccer has no borders, these scandals have emerged cyclically and consistently in Italian soccer history. Corruption scandals involving the country's 'power field' do not seem to deeply shake national sensibilities and ideals about the ethics of Italian society, let alone soccer, which has arguably reflected Italy's virtues and vices since its origin.

This chapter will focus on the increasingly important role that corruption as *doxa* – logic or rules of the game – plays within the Italian soccer 'field'. The chapter starts by focusing on the concept of *scandal* as a social phenomenon, tracing its origins and moving to its current traits. After having clarified this concept, the chapter will examine major Italian soccer corruption scandals, setting the context for chapters 4 and 5 and their analysis on the involvement of the mafias in soccer.

Scandal as a 'trial': a sociological sketch

Scandals as social phenomena have consistently been the focus of sociological investigations for the last 20 years. This attention is due to the frequent use of the term 'scandal' by the media in relation to diverse 'wrongdoings', including serious crimes and corruption. When focusing on scandals, the emphasis is directed at the same time to society's morality and social order. This is due to the historical and symbolic meaning of the concept of scandal. The term has been used by different societies throughout history. Ancient Romans used the term 'scandalum' to indicate a temptation, a stumbling block; in the 1600s, the French term 'scandale' indicated discredit caused by irregular conduct.[2] It is in this latter meaning and with the advent of Christianity that the negative connotation of the term and its link to morality consolidated. The term is mentioned in the Gospels of Matthew; Matthew writes: "Necesse est enim ut veniant scandal [plural of scandalum]; verumtamen vae homini per quem scandalum venit" [*Indeed it is inevitable that scandals occur, but woe to the man by whose fault the scandal occurs*;18.7].[3] Matthew's statement underlines the ability of scandals to reveal what is considered by Christianity as the sinful nature of humans and the need for redemption.

The connection of the concept of scandal to morality is important not only for Christianity but also for any socio-cultural analysis of the phenomenon. French sociologist Emile Durkheim's work on moral order (1912) provides a convincing frame to understand the social dimension of scandals. When scandals occur, they put the dominant moral order in the spotlight; they indicate which behaviours are considered the norm and which should be chastised – in religious terms, which norms are 'sacred' and must not be violated and which are 'profane' (Durkheim in Jacobsson and Löfmarck, 2008).[4]

Scandals represented by the media aim to provoke collective reaction, as public, shared norms have been violated; in Durkheimian terms, transgressing shared norms undermines collective identity and social cohesion (Jacobsson and Löfmarck, 2008). A good example of this dynamic at play is given by the recent soccer World Cup bidding scandal; in 2017, the media highlighted a FIFA ethics report stating that the Duke of Cambridge and former UK Prime Minister David Cameron allegedly attended a meeting involving a vote-swapping deal between England and South Korea. The media stated that when David Cameron asked the South Korean representatives to support England for the 2018 World Cup bid, he was allegedly asked to reciprocate in the following 2022 bid, in violation of the FIFA anti-collusion rules (*The Telegraph* – online, 2017). English former striker and BBC presenter Gary Lineker immediately commented: "The FIFA bidding process created a murky world where favours/bribes were just thrown around."[5]

In this case, the scandal challenged the international soccer system's moral order, creating an impulse for a moralising process – as moral order values/norms needed to be reinforced. The moral norms pertinent to soccer, and any other sports, are encompassed by the notion of 'fair play' (Loland and McNamee, 2000), which formally rules how the game should be regulated and informally provides for those 'dispositions', which are best characterised by doing one's best and respecting one's opponents. The World Cup scandal[6] revealed instead a tacit and widely diffused *doxa* about how soccer should be run, which are in stark contrast to the more publicly shared and widely promoted 'fair play' ideals.

The resulting public outcry after appearances in the news of scandals is generally followed by moral preaching and lessons to be learned. Scandals show, in this sense, their ritual nature, aiming to reinforce dominant collective values while at the same time serving a communicative aim to be "analogous to culturally produced texts" that can be systematically read to endow "meaning upon experience" (Turner, 1967, p. 30 in de Blic and Lemieux, 2005). These 'texts' remind the collective how social relationships should be regulated and the values on which they should be founded.

American sociologist Erving Goffman and his frame analysis provides another intriguing understanding of scandals. For Goffman (1986) the self is the individual we present to others during daily interactions, which Goffman sees as theatrical plays; the self is put forth towards others almost as if playing a character. Life is like a theatre where plays are staged; individuals exercise choices on what they perceive within the play – they give meanings to speeches and behaviours by choosing what they want to perceive. During these 'performances', the self is constructed; people or actors are successful if they convince others they are who and what they claim to be (Ritzer and Stepnisky, 2017). For instance, the scandal mentioned previously involving the president of the Real Federación Española de Fútbol, according to Goffman's frame, would represent a desecration of the founding values of soccer and sport and deviance from the accepted way of behaving. The dogma of sport as fair and most importantly 'clean' from corruption is challenged by the scandal, and the behaviour is chastised, as it involves breaking the norms of the conduct that the frame of reference imposes. Angel Maria Villar represents, in this sense, the whole Spanish soccer establishment, its normative and ethical authority, its players, coaches and fans, and therefore he embodies trust. His alleged violation is a defilement of what is sacred for many Spanish soccer fans.

Mediated scandals are also social dramas (Turner, 1982 in Kantola and Vesa, 2013) following a script; they have four phases: in phase one there is a violation of a norm/value, which is considered collectively crucial in regulating social relations; in phase two, there is a crisis which widens; in phase three redressing is carried out; and finally in phase four, there is a reintegration of the "disturbed social group or, alternatively, the recognition of an irreparable schism" (Turner, 1988, 1974 in Kantola and Vesa, 2013, p. 296).

From a Bourdieuian lens, as scandals violate the 'sacred', which represents the collective and regulates social relations in a field, while provoking a strong collective reaction, they should also be the occasion to promote a crisis of the status quo of the field where they occur. They should stimulate 'reflexivity', favouring change or a revalidation of the *doxa* of the field; this process may at the same time shape the *habitus* by promoting resistance to the status quo or its alignment to the *doxa* of the field. Hence, scandals are sociologically relevant because they can provide insights into how influential they are in promoting social change.

French sociologist Eric de Dampierre's idea of scandal as test is valuable here and compatible with Bourdieu's praxeology. De Dampierre argues:

The test is about transgressed values, [. . .] to assess if the collective has become indifferent to them. In relation to this function, the most significant outcomes are the confirmation of the transgressed values as current and the society/collective demand that the offenders are punished, or the 'implicit' acknowledgement that the episode is a non-scandal via the generalisation of the denounced offense.

(de Blic and Lemieux, 2005, p. 4)

Italian corruption cases, their impacts and diffusion in several fields of the Italian social space – including soccer – seem to confirm the 'non-scandal' hypothesis, and certainly they play a role in contributing to international media coverage, which ranges from bewildering to ironic.

Italian soccer style: the context

In 2017, a survey from the poll firm Demopolis reported that 48% of Italians believed that corruption was more diffused and 42% believed that it was unchanged if compared with the 'Tangentopoli' scandal in 1992.[7] The Director of Transparency International-Italia argues that corruptive practices are widespread because of their symbolic power; they are linked with successful and powerful people:

> If people see that the representatives of the power system [what Bourdieu would term as power field, and that includes politicians, high bureaucrats, businessmen and other powerful figures in any Italian field, including soccer] who corrupt or are corrupted have success, they start to realize that it is worth risking it; corruption-related practices are so predominant in Italy that there is no way for individuals and organisations to escape being involved in these dynamics.[8]

The location-status of the social actor in any field – including soccer – coupled with an unconscious internalisation that corruption is the rule and unavoidable, may contribute to the seriality of the practice and also its diffusion in soccer. The director of the Italian branch of Transparency International adds:

If a person needs to wait ages to carry out an important health checkup with the national health service and he/she is able to do it in one week via recommendation, if a person needs an important document given by the local authority but he/she knows it is difficult to obtain it even if he/she is entitled to it and can resolve the problem by paying someone, corrupt practices become widespread and corruption as logic in dealing with the power system becomes normalised, no longer being seen as a wrong-doing but as a necessity.[9]

This habituation to corrupt practices is shown by the Demopolis survey findings; it also brings about a tacit sense of inevitability in the way Italians seem to perceive corruption. Although cases of corrupt practices occur in any country in the world, this level of tolerance seems quite significant in Italy, as the director of the Italian branch of Transparency International affirmed.

Corradino (Italian Anti-Corruption Agency – ANAC) is able to capture this idea of corruption as a habitual practice for the corruptors, for the corrupted and, worryingly, for the public:

> Recently, the judiciary and police have uncovered a welfare model based on corruption which provides a golden handshake when the corrupted does not want to be involved in the network of power anymore; he/she is paid a pension! And when during the investigation prosecutors asked why this occurred, the offenders (corruptors) replied that they wanted to reassure the other actors of the network about its credibility. What is more surprising is that many of these people were not those who directly committed the corrupt activities, but instead they were put at the service of the businessmen, always ready when needed; their function was not so much to commit corrupt acts but to connect businesses with the members of the PA [public administrator], who will be corrupted in the future. I was stunned by some wiretappings in which a CEO of a small business was earning €2000 a month, but was obliged to give €5000 to one of these dodgy dealmakers as commission. The person was acting as a financial broker who would contact a corrupt public administrator [who was also paid].[10]

It would be naïve to think that the soccer field does not reflect these dynamics. In 2016, the Italian polling agency Demos (*La Repubblica* – online, 2016) surveyed Italian soccer fans to provide an analytical snapshot of the Italian soccer state of affairs. Among the findings, the fans' attitude on the lack of credibility of Italian soccer emerged. Illegal betting and corruption scandals had dented the trust of Italian fans in the country's most popular sport. Only 2 out of 10 fans thought that Italian soccer was now more credible than 10 years ago; the current president of the Italian Football (soccer) Federation was deemed untrustworthy; 9 out of 10 fans wanted scrutiny via technological support during soccer matches as a deterrent to match-fixing. The fans also agreed that after the latest soccer scandals, nothing had changed, and in fact corruption had worsened.

In Italy, soccer is a €1.9 billion business within Europe's €25 billion market (*Il Sole 24 Ore* – online, 2017). Italian soccer is an industry which produces wealth and many job opportunities via TV rights, sponsors, merchandising and marketing players. The hyper-commercialisation of soccer has negative effects, as it creates enormous costs: many teams are now in the stock market, and the teams' expenses must conform to pre-established budgets. This situation is probably one of the reasons why the main Italian teams – with the exception of Juventus FC and ACF Fiorentina – have been the object of foreign investments. AS Roma, AC Milan and FC Inter Milan currently have foreign presidents and ownerships. The soccer of the past, when rich businessmen such as Gianni Agnelli (Juventus FC) were able to buy clubs and manage them, is indeed in the past; many Italian tycoons do not consider it worth investing in soccer just for reasons of ego and status. This commitment would be not only financially onerous but also psychologically exhausting, as it also demands dealing with the daily hassles of well-organised and often violent hard-core fans (Ultras) who will criticise the club management for on- and off-pitch activities. In fact, Italian soccer is undergoing a deep crisis, which symbolically was highlighted in November 2017 when the 'Azzurri' (Italian national team and quadruple World Cup holder) did not qualify to participate in the FIFA World Cup hosted by Russia in summer 2018; this has not occurred since 1958 (*The Huffington Post* – online, 2017).[11]

There is also an imbalance between the rich Lega Serie A (the top division, premier league) and the lower divisions, including the Lega Serie B and the minor leagues, which are poorly controlled by the Italian soccer authorities, and for this reason are more prone to corruption and violations of sporting rules. The Lega Serie B authority has complained – rightly so – several times about its lack of power to control who purchases soccer clubs, and this was emphasised by the director of the media relations office of the Lega Serie B to the authors of this book:

> The organisation had put forward a proposal for reform to the Italian soccer federation in order to be able to adopt regulations which allow preventative control of the financial solidity, background and reputation of those interested in the purchase of a soccer club before it occurs.[12]

This request is reasonable, and it is perplexing how this scrutiny function has not been given to the Lega Serie B until now, especially considering that in Italy, as with mainstream corruption, soccer corruption scandals seem to promote only obliviousness and an unconscious collective internalisation that corruption seems to have become a rule of the game too lucrative for predatory individuals and groups such as mafia clans not to be involved.

Scandals of Italian soccer: match-fixing, corruption and social dramas

Historically, Italian soccer has often been considered the most successful in the world; however, this 'pedigree' has been tainted by a history of 'scandals', which consistently – since 1927 – have been reported by Italian media (Vignati, 2016). In 1927, the first major scandal involved the successful FC Torino and its management. Mr Nani, manager of FC Torino, contacted the Juventus defender Luigi Allemandi and asked him to favour the victory of the FC Torino in exchange for 50,000 Lire (equivalent to approx. €56,000).[13] On June 5, 1927, Torino FC won the match against Juventus FC; however, Allemandi was one of the best players of the match, and because of this, Nani refused to pay him the money. When subsequently they met, an argument ensued and was overheard by an Italian journalist, who published the story. Even though the Italian soccer federation did not find evidence of match-fixing, Nani and Allemandi were barred from soccer for life, and the 'scudetto' ('Italian Serie A' championship title), won by FC Torino, was annulled.[14]

As Vignati (2016) points out, the 1940s/50s were plagued by many more soccer scandals involving all three Italian soccer divisions. A significant one occurred in Serie C (the third division) in season 1948–1949, when Catania FC and Avellino FC, two southern regional teams, were accused of cheating. The play-off was won by Avellino FC 1–0; however, the management of Catania FC reported the match to the police, stating that Avellino FC had paid Stabia FC to lose a match against them. During investigations, other rumours about match-fixing emerged involving all the division's southern teams. The Italian soccer authorities promptly annulled all the matches involving southern teams and relegated Avellino FC and Catania FC to the lower division.[15]

Clearly, in soccer, corruption scandals do not take place only in the south, as history shows. During the 1954–1955 season, the northern Udinese FC, which had reached the second place in the Lega Serie A, was investigated by soccer authorities on suspicion of match-fixing. During investigations, the Italian soccer federation proved that a match played during the 1952–1953 season against Pro Patria FC was fixed, resulting in Udinese FC being relegated to Lega Serie B; in the same season, Catania FC was also relegated to Lega Serie B because one of the management members corrupted the referee, who was barred from soccer for life (*Il Giornale* – online, 2006).

It was during the 1980s, however, that the major scandal known as 'Calcio-Scommesse' (Soccer Bets) became notorious worldwide and tainted Italy's reputation in a period where 'made in Italy' was at the pinnacle of its world popularity. On March 23, 1980, the Italian police broke onto the soccer pitches during Lega Serie A and B championships in various Italian cities and arrested several players. The episode was aired live during the TV Broadcast 'Novantesimo Minuto' – a popular Italian Sunday television programme on air since the 1970s (Vignati, 2016). Thirteen players and the presidents of AC Milan and SS Lazio were arrested, and 50 players were investigated by the judiciary. The criminal and disciplinary proceedings started almost immediately, and whilst the criminal proceedings ended with no convictions, the sport disciplinary proceedings were more incisive: SS Lazio and Milan FC were relegated to Lega Serie B, and Avellino FC, Bologna FC and Perugia FC were penalised five points. The president of AC Milan was disbarred, while the Bologna FC president was punished with one year of disqualification, and 17 players of several clubs were suspended for periods of three months to six years. This major scandal, though, did not prevent the 'Azzurri' (the national team) from winning the 1982 FIFA World Cup, providing Italian soccer worldwide redemption. After this time, the Italian soccer federation decided on an amnesty for nine players. who subsequently retired.[16]

During the season 1999–2000, Italian soccer fans read once more in the papers about another scandal – the so-called 'Rolex' affair, with reference to the famous Swiss brand of watches. The story involved the president of AS Roma, who gave 25 gold Rolex watches as Christmas presents to referees of Lega Serie A and B, disregarding the fact that the Italian soccer federation and Lega Serie A considered this practice rightly inappropriate. The president of the Lega Serie A, Franco Carraro, stated to journalists that it was a very serious episode.[17] It is also worth noting that Franco Carraro, former mayor of Rome and a national politician, six years later, as president of the Italian Soccer Federation, was also involved in another scandal. In that case, one of his phone conversations with Paolo Bergamo – the soccer officer who selected referees – was wiretapped while he asked Bergamo not to disadvantage SS Lazio. Carraro was suspended for four years and six months by the Italian soccer federation Court of Appeal and received an €80,000 fine in the federal court, but at the criminal trial, the judge for the preliminary hearing in Naples (GUP) in 2009 acquitted him from the charges of sports fraud due to insufficient evidence, a decision which was also confirmed by the Italian Court of Cassation (*Il Fatto Quotidiano* – online, 2013).[18]

The Rolex scandal uncovered to Italian fans, and the wider public, the diffusion of a tacit, unethical practice of giving expensive presents across the industry. Although no criminal offence was proved, the episode encouraged fans' suspicions about the ease in 'buying' Italian soccer referees. In 2016, a Demos survey reported that Italian fans identified diffused corruption as being the major culprits in Italian soccer's lack of credibility.[19]

In the same year, 2000, Italian soccer was again in the media spotlight for the wrong reasons. This time, the scandal was called by the Italian media 'Passoportopoli' (City of Passports) due to fake passports being issued to several foreign players in violation of the Italian soccer federation article 40, which forbids soccer teams to deploy more than five non-EU players. The teams involved in the violation were treated leniently by Italian soccer authorities, avoiding the financial disaster of relegation to lower divisions, but they were economically sanctioned, and their soccer players disqualified. The proverbial 'straw that broke the camel's back' occurred on September 14, 2000: three players of Udinese FC were stopped by the police and their passports discovered as fake.[20] As with all Italian scandals, Passoportopoli widened its reach, uncovering a corruption-based 'system' in place, involving other teams (Inter Milan FC, AC Milan, SS Lazio, AS Roma, Udinese FC, Vicenza FC and Sampdoria FC) and well-known players such as Uruguayan Alvaro Recoba and Argentinean Juan Sebastián Verón. On May 3, 2001, article 40 was 'conveniently' modified by the Italian soccer federation in favour of the deployment of more non-EU players. Inter Milan FC was ordered to pay a 2 billion Lire sanction (equivalent to approx. €1,3 billion[21]), and Recoba and other players were disqualified for one year.[22] In 2006, the Italian courts sentenced Recoba and the Inter Milan manager and former Italian national winner of the 1982 World Cup Lele Oriali to six months' imprisonment, then replaced this with a fine of €21,420 for the offence of forging an official document and receiving stolen goods (*La Gazzetta dello Sport* – online, 2006).

Six years later, corruption, as *doxa* of the Italian soccer field, emerged again. In 2007, newspapers *La Repubblica* and *La Gazzetta dello Sport* began to publish wiretaps by the Italian police, which uncovered a major corruption-led system dubbed 'Calciopoli'(City of Soccer). The wiretaps detailed the attempt of club managers to influence the choice of the referees for the matches. The sport disciplinary proceedings mostly focused on the powerful Juventus manager Luciano Moggi, a figure that fits well with the 'dealmaker' sketched by Corradino (ANAC) in chapter 2 of this book. The investigations of the judiciary demonstrated how Moggi was able to manipulate the selection of referees and coverage of the TV matches, even through choosing more Juventus FC-friendly journalists. For the Italian Supreme Court, Moggi was a novel Machiavellian Prince, "the creator of a corrupt-led system which aimed to influence the soccer matches for the season 2004–2005 and beyond" (*La Repubblica* – online, 2015). The judicial proceedings once more showed that soccer mirrored the broader corruption issue in Italian society.

While other clubs (AC Milan, Fiorentina FC, SS Lazio and Reggina FC) were involved, Juventus FC was punished hard. The prosecution argued that Juventus FC, nicknamed 'Vecchia Signora' (Old Lady), was the only team that set out to deliberately alter the outcome of the matches. Fiorentina FC and SS Lazio were initially relegated to the lower division, but those decisions were later reversed in favour of their expulsion from European competitions. Juventus FC was relegated to Lega Serie B, their Lega Serie A title was annulled for seasons 2004–2005 and 2005–2006 (*La Stampa* – online, 2015), and they were penalised nine points for season 2006–2007. Sanctions such as fines, penalisation points, and home fixtures played with no public viewings were also given to AC Milan, SS Lazio and Reggina FC for the season 2005–2006. Since 2016, Moggi has received numerous sanctions given by both the sport and justice system: he was barred for life in 2011, and this was upheld in 2017 by the administrative appeal court, the Consiglio di Stato – Council of State (*La Gazzetta dello Sport* – online, 2017).

As Italian history shows, major corruption scandals emerge cyclically – in 2011, 'Operation Last Bet' hit all the major newspapers' first pages: 120 individuals under investigation and 54 arrested, among whom were players and managers of Serie A, B and Lega Pro (contemporary name for the third division) teams. The investigation started when the goalkeeper of Cremonese FC, Marco Paoloni, was accused of providing his team members with an anti-anxiolytic drug in order to lose a match.[23] Last Bet revealed the same sophistication found in Italian mainstream corruption scandals, this time applied to 'adjusting' the results of soccer matches. Having as accomplices specific team players made 'adjusting' matches easier; goalkeepers, strikers and defenders were crucial. A conversation between Paoloni and a journalist is quite revealing:

> I have 'adjusted' dozens of matches when I was on the pitch, and other matches when I did not play. It was easier to corrupt Italians than foreigners. . . . The first contact with the clan (criminal network) was like a romantic courtship; we met for dinners four or five times, the aim was to explain what we needed to do. They [the network] bet on specific platforms from Asia; this method aims to avoid being traced as the abnormal flow of money is not identifiable. They bet 'live' only during the match.
>
> (*La Gazzetta dello Sport* – online, 2015)

Last Bet also uncovered these 'practices' in the soccer youth division. One player filmed a meeting with a team manager where he was asked to 'adjust' a result, as the transcribed conversation shows:

MANAGER: Saturday I will give you €500, and then if you do as explained [on Sunday], on Monday I will give you €1000.
PLAYER: Not enough; for this amount of money, I will not do it; to lose the match I want €5000.
MANAGER: Let's do €3000 and stop busting my balls![24]

Intimidation and violence were also part of the 'game'; those who did not want to carry out illicit deeds were threatened. A phone conversation wiretapped between a player and an angry betting punter regarding a goalkeeper who did not comply shows this dynamic:

PLAYER: This [goalkeeper] does not deserve to be shot but to be beaten up till he dies.
PUNTER: Kill him; OK, bring him here so that we will kill him.[25]

Another conversation detailed the owner of a betting shop threatening the same goalkeeper: "He must die if he has done it – he jeopardises everyone, he has to give our money back."[26]

Intimidation or violence could be avoided only when punters recovered the money loss via the 'adjusting' of another match or when the non-complying players accepted written cheques to guarantee the result. If the 'issue' was not resolved, kidnapping was one of the answers; the following excerpt explains this dynamic: "He has taken so much beating; now we are bringing him to the countryside. He does not have money, he said that yesterday he lost again. That he needs more time."[27]

In this context, the notorious Italian hard-core fans known as *Ultras* may be involved, often to threaten players and make them lose the matches on which they bet. Two players were phone wiretapped by the police when speaking about their relationship with the Ultras:

PLAYER 1: They told me that the Ultras went to the players saying '. . . now you have busted our balls, you have been relegated [lower division]; now you must lose the next two matches.
PLAYER 2: So when this occurs, what do you do? You do as you're told because if I threaten them saying I will report this to the federal sport attorney's office, they will come to 'pick me up' at my house [the violence overtone here is clear].

(*Il Corriere della Sera* – online, 2004)

Ultras are not only present in corruption scandals; indeed, some groups may also be linked to mafia clans, for whom they might represent foot soldiers. The Italian Direzione Investigativa Antimafia[28] (DIA) has repeatedly stressed this link. In 2006 during the match Arzanese FC vs Afragolese FC, the supporters of the Arzanese displayed a banner which paid tribute to the President of the Afragolese, who was a leader of the Camorra clan Moccia from the town of Afragola (near Naples) – and as if that was not enough, the management of the Arzanese gave him a bunch of flowers.[29]

The link between the camorra clans and Ultras is also present in the historical San Paolo Stadium terraces in Naples: Ultras groups which are linked with rival camorra clans are separated in the stadium to prevent violent outbursts. The DIA mentioned the statements of the cooperating witness and former member of the Misso clan from the Rione Sanità (district Sanità in Naples), who argued:

In the [soccer] terraces the laws of the camorra rule . . . it is evident that if fans from the 'Quartieri Spagnoli' [notorious district in Central Naples] and of the historic centre of the city were connected with the Misso clan, they could not interact with those fans linked to the Licciardi clan from Secondigliano [town near Naples].[30]

The DIA also points out how easy it is to identify the affiliation of these fans to camorra clans from their banners; the banner 'Masseria Cardone' [Masseria is a group of no more than 80 hard-core fans] indicates the link to the Licciardi clan, while the banner of the 'Teste Matte' [Crazy Heads] refers to the Quartieri Spagnoli clan of Naples.[31]

The last two soccer scandals show not only the popularity of matchfixing but also the extent of corruption as a *doxa*, which in its diffusion, internalisation and normalisation is also found in major scandals involving the Italian power field at the national, regional and metropolitan levels. It also stresses that hard-core fan groups are characters of these recurring Italian 'social dramas'.

Soccer's corruptive practices and the 'Bel Paese'

From the scandals so far analysed, and drawing from Di Ronco and Lavorgna's (2015) typology of soccer 'wrongdoings' in Italy, it is possible to identify four manifestations of corruption-led practices in soccer in the 'Bel Paese' (the lush place – Italy's nickname).

The first typology focuses on the relationship between owners or managers of soccer clubs and public officials; this type is exemplified by an instance occurring in 2010 involving local politician David Codognotto, the commissioner for sport of the town of 'San Michele del Tagliamento' who was sent to jail because he extorted €15,000 from the CEO of FC Portosummaga, a soccer team playing in Serie B. Codognotto asked for the money from the sport club Lemene owned by Portosummaga; in return Codognotto would have authorised regional funding of €90,000 to finance the youth championships. In 2014 the Italian court of appeal of the city of Venice upheld the local politician's sentence to two years and eight months' imprisonment.[32]

Codognotto's case is only one example of the inventiveness of corrupt Italian politicians and bureaucrats; in other cases, the kickbacks are disguised as sponsorship for locally funded municipal soccer teams. As mentioned earlier, this sophistication reflects exactly what occurs in the country outside of the soccer field. In Italy, corruption-related practices have become so sophisticated that it is difficult to understand the systems even when perceived or uncovered. Michele Corradino (ANAC) explains this perennial mutation well:

> We have different levels of corruption; criminal corruption is changing in our country. We are witnessing a process of dematerialisation of the bribe on the one hand, and on the other, the emergence of the new figure of dodgy dealmakers – individuals who are also heavily present in soccer, as the Calciopoli scandal showed. It is increasingly difficult and complex to identify corruption, because the classic model of corruption based on the exchange of a price for a service/ favour is increasingly replaced by the sophisticated payment of kickbacks. They move the money around in very creative ways, even hiding it in very strange places – inside sofas, in the fridge, freezer, etc. . . . but money continues to circulate. We are also witnessing new types of bribes, such as a judge allegedly asking for breast surgery for his lover! Funny situation aside, current data tells us that new type of bribes are used, from obtaining free mozzarella to getting a complete service that helps the corrupt individual with all his/her problems; there are extremes where someone has also asked to have a lifelong supply of toilet tissue![33]

The second typology of wrongdoing emerging in Italian soccer is represented by fraudulent bankruptcy, which is prohibited by Italian Law no. 267/1942. A recent case (2017) of fraudulent bankruptcy has involved Siena Calcio FC. The Guardia di Finanza (Italian financial police) seized €8.5 million from the former president of the club, who allegedly misappropriated club money and falsified club account figures. In 2017, a similar case involved another reasonably well-known soccer team, FC Ravenna. In this case, the club management declared bankruptcy in 2012 and was allegedly accused of declaring fictitious sponsorships as well as conducting a series of fake operations to show a positive balance sheet (*Il Resto del Carlino*, 2017). This type of illicit activity also involves the corruption of accountants and other public officials or is linked to a system that aims to move proceeds of corruption abroad, as reflected by the 2.5-year sentence of given by the Genova city tribunal to the former President of the Lucchese Libertas Calcio 1905, Syrian businessman Hadj Ahmad Fouzi, who was accused of both fraudulent bankruptcy of the soccer club and international corruption (*Il Secolo XIX* – online, 2015).

Money laundering is also significantly present in Italy, as well as at the European level. The Organization for Security and Co-operation in Europe (OCSE) as early as 2009 stressed how European soccer was vulnerable to money laundering in two different ways: as a means used by individuals involved in soccer to avoid taxes and as a means for mafias to invest 'dirty' money in legitimate businesses (*La Repubblica* – online, 2009). In chapters 4 and 5, we will focus on the latter. For the moment, it suffices to say that in 2014, the Italian newsmagazine *L'Espresso* interviewed an agent of various Italian soccer players who underlined the existence of an international network of lawyers able to set up offshore businesses to send part of the money gained from soccer players' transfers. He argued:

> The clubs that 'own' the players receive money from the buyer club for the transfer of the player, but withhold a part of it. So in fact, the player is valued at less money than the media claims because part of the total money is given to the player's agents and managers. So, by magic, that money escapes the Italian tax system.[34]

The third typology is indicated by the findings of operation 'Last Bet' which has once more brought to the attention of the fans and the public the crime of illegal betting, which is prohibited in Italy by Law 401/1989,[35] with a sentence of up to three years' imprisonment. We have explained the dynamics of illegal betting in Italy earlier in the chapter; however, it is important to point out that this typology of corruption-led practices does not only occur in Italy. In 2013, Germany, a country considered virtuous in terms of corruption cases and prevention,[36] was at the centre of a major Europol investigation which uncovered a network of illegal betting based in Asia and that may have 'adjusted' 380 matches in Europe and 300 matches across Africa, Asia and Latin America, including qualification matches for both the World Cup and UEFA Cup and matches in the UK Champions league.[37]

The fourth typology is represented by match-fixing, which tends to be one of the most recurrent corrupt practices in Italian soccer in lower divisions as well as youth soccer, where there is less scrutiny by the media and soccer authorities. A recent survey of the agency Demos (2016)[38] shows that 1 in 2 Italian supporters believed that soccer was conditioned by betting, and 1 in 4 by corruption, while 31% of the participants believed that soccer was conditioned by mafia power.

The same public perception of the inevitability of corruption is experienced among soccer fans, and possibly internalised among the social actors involved in Italian soccer from the beginning of either their careers or involvement in soccer. Corradino mentioned various episodes which highlight how 'la raccomandazione', for instance, may be as much a part of the Italian youth soccer scene as it is in mainstream society. For example, in one instance a father (and president of the soccer team where his son was playing) allegedly paid the coach to ensure his son would be playing in the match. In another instance, 'la raccomandazione' features in a case involving a soccer player who was sanctioned by the Italian soccer authorities for match-fixing and disqualified – he contacted his father and asked him to use his influential friendship to limit the disqualification only to one match, and promptly obtained his desired outcome.[39]

The inevitability of corruption in soccer seems to be shared also by some Italian soccer players. Recent research of Transparency International – Italia (2014),[40] aiming to understand soccer players' views on the relationship between sport and ethics and the problem of match-fixing, surveyed soccer players and staff of the Lega Serie B. The findings are particularly revealing, as the causes of corruption/match-fixing were identified in how soccer as a 'field' is structured, in its inefficiency and in the negative role models provided by those who run and are part of the sport. The generalized criminal interests were identified as a major cause by 63% of participants, while 42% pointed out a lack of morality in Italian society as a whole. The lower divisions were identified as the core of the problem (90%). In common with surveys dealing with mainstream corruption-related practices, 100% of the participants perceived corruption as society's 'virus', which infested soccer as well. This result can be understood when realising how many of those at the top of the Italian soccer industry are also part of the country's power field as politicians, high-ranking bureaucrats and businessmen. The general perception of the players was that match-fixing, and more generally corruption in soccer, will increase and become more evident in the future; 60% of the participants indicated that if something is not done to address it, it will rise, while 20% of participants think it will stay the same. It is also important to stress how mafias are considered one of the main causes for match-fixing: 60% believed that this was the case.

As mentioned in the survey, others' behaviours play an important part in the perception of the players in relation to match-fixing, so well-known players have a role – as they are taken as examples by the wider public – in breaking the perception of impotence and inevitability of corruption. Sometimes this narrative of resistance to the status quo is put forward, and sometimes this is less evident. In 2012, Luigi Buffon's interview with the Italian newspaper *La Gazzetta dello Sport* was certainly not helpful; Buffon – goalkeeper and world champion with the Italian team that won the World Cup of 2006 – is a soccer player renowned internationally for his skills and for his honesty; however, although clearly condemning match-fixing in an interview, he controversially argued:

> There are matches at the end of the season when for both teams a draw is fine [useful] to avoid relegation to a lower division; what do you ask for? Who will explain this to the fans [in case one team plays to win or lose the match]?
>
> (*La Gazzetta dello Sport* – online, 2012)

The equation 'wider corruption in society with wider corruption in sport/soccer' is controversial. Hill (2013) argues that if this equivalence was true, a virtuous country (in relation to the Transparency International Corruption Perception Index) such as Singapore should express a virtuous soccer scene; however, he affirms, this is not the case. While Declan focuses on society, it might be more revealing to focus on the country's power field. If this field has as its main logic corruption and unethical behaviours, this *modus operandi* is likely to be reflected in all other fields of national relevance, including soccer. The well-established connection, power field–mafia, is also reflected in the connection soccer–mafia, which is becoming evident day after day.

Lastly, there is an issue with the inefficiency of both the ordinary and the sport judiciary systems, as also pointed out by Transparency International-Italia (2014) among the causes of match-fixing. In this study, 50% of the respondents mentioned the Italian legislation as lacking any deterrence function, while 70% pointed out the limitations of the sport legislation providing for too lenient sanctions while it should instead advocate for the expulsion from soccer of those involved in match-fixing. The inefficiency of both ordinary and sport law is leading to what Di Ronco and Lavorgna (2015) identify as 'hubs of criminal opportunities', as it involves the lack of *ad hoc* laws, poor control over power (in this case over Italian soccer authorities), poor control and lack of transparency on how soccer is financed and increasing discretion on how teams are managed, especially in lower and amateur divisions.

The Lega Serie B is working to improve legislation and control mechanisms in its soccer clubs. The aim is not to be passive 'spectators' but to act. In 2017, the Lega Serie B proposed a bill to the Italian government to allow for the seizure of assets of soccer players who are involved in illicit activities and corruption cases. A representative of the Lega Serie B argues.

Whoever commits these criminal acts will understand that the LEGA does not give him shelter; we will be relentless: 'you play, you pay'. These actions should not only concern sport justice; for whoever is guilty of corruption, both criminal and civil, justice must act immediately.[41]

We can agree with the Lega Serie B about the need to improve current legislation; the focus should be to clarify the boundaries of sport justice in relation to ordinary jurisdiction – the state judiciary. Law 280/2003 outlines that the state acknowledges the autonomy of the sport judiciary system as an autonomous justice system. It follows that ordinary judiciary intervenes only when all degrees of sport justice have terminated and when the matter is related to patrimonial matters.[42] As antimafia legislation has been built as a double-track system – complementary and in a relationship of specialisation from ordinary criminal jurisdiction – and the antimafia code (legislative decree 159/2011) is heavily invested in ruling for confiscation and patrimonial provisions, a more formalised interaction across sport justice and antimafia should be desirable if not obvious.

The improvement of the law should be combined with more control of the relevant soccer authorities at national and divisional levels. The Lega Serie B is working in this direction, but more needs to be done. In particular, the soccer divisions' authorities, especially those overseeing the amateur and youth divisions, must intensify efforts by organising meetings with youth and team players, but also the legal sector, betting control agencies and players who have acted as whistle-blowers, thus focusing on the risks and negative impacts of these crimes for the sport and for who is involved. At the same time, Italian soccer authorities must educate the youth (and players in general) to respect the regulations and to conform to behaviours which are based on the principles of legality and fair play.

In conclusion, the recurrence of soccer 'scandals' in Italy can be considered symptomatic of the inability of the soccer authorities to ensure transparency and accountability. These scandals show that corrupt practices are as serial and widespread in Italian soccer as in society in general. As corruption is an intrinsic character of mafia power, soccer, hence, provides fertile ground for mafia power to prosper.

In particular, it is the notion of consensus that anchors mafia power not only to the territory – local and national – but also, and especially, to the people in that territory. Consensus within the mafia 'field' does not mean conscious or even voluntary approval of certain (illegal/illicit/condemnable) behaviours, but rather co-existence with, and normalisation of, those behaviours. This can happen at various degrees of awareness, and it gives birth to hybrid types of social interactions.

Before moving to the next chapter, which will look at the relationship between both mafia and soccer fields more closely, a preliminary and fundamental distinction must be made between territories where mafia *doxa* are physically and socially entrenched and recognised as such (we would call them 'traditional' or 'original' mafia areas) and territories of mafia migration and further settlement (we can call them 'non-traditional' or 'derivative' mafia areas) where *doxa* are present but less likely to be recognised.

In the first case, in 'traditional/original' mafia areas (villages and towns of regions like Calabria, Sicily, the hinterland of Campania), the knowledge of who belongs to a family identified as a mafia family is often paired with frequent links with that family – such as encounters in social and communal occasions, such as church, school, soccer pitches, even the supermarket or the post office. Frequency of daily life, together with a classification of certain phenomena as 'normal' – as in expected, ordinary, for that place or group of people – makes the mafia phenomenon in certain territories almost invisible in its entirety and as such *tolerable*. This is the social space where symbols, practices, traditions and rituals meet with mafia practices. Within such social space, *habitus* – a sense of one's place and a sense of the place of others – is formed and shaped. Mafia organisations in this context function as total institutions (Bourdieu and Passeron, 1990), and soccer becomes one of the most effective means to gain economic, symbolic and social capital, important for the mafias to maintain power, social control and consensus.

Notes

1 'Calcio scandalo in Toscana'; cf. www.primapaginachiusi.it/2017/07/calcio-scandalo-toscana-agli-arresti-il-presidente-della-sestese-la-squadra-che-affosso-il-chiusiimmigrazione-clandestina-documenti-falsi-frode-sporiva/; www.arezzonotizie.it/cronaca/presunte-combine-nei-dilettanti-lelenco-dei-match-sospetti/
2 Cf. www.etymonline.com/index.php?term=scandal&allowed_in_frame=0
3 Cf. www.treccani.it/vocabolario/necesse-est-enim-ut-veniant-scandala/
4 Cf. Durkheim, http://home.ku.edu.tr/~mbaker/cshs503/durkheimreligiouslife.pdf
5 'Former PM David Cameron and Prince William Embroiled in Football World Cup Bidding Scandal'; cf. http://uk.businessinsider.com/david-cameron-and-princewilliam-embroiled-in-football-world-cup-bidding-scandal-2017-6
6 Cf. chapter 2 of this book.
7 'Demopolis: la corruzione in Italia, 25 anni dopo l'inchiesta di Mani Pulite'; cf. www.demopolis.it/?p=3884

Scandals, the 'sins' and 'sinners' of soccer 79

8 Excerpt 5 interview DM (2017).
9 Excerpt 15 interview DM (2017).
10 Excerpt 21 interview C (2017).
11 'World Cup 2018: Where Did It All Go Wrong for Italy?' Cf. www.bbc. co.uk/sport/football/41977785
12 Excerpt 10 interview LSB (2017).
13 www.infodata.ilsole24ore.com/2015/04/14/se-potessi-avere-calcola-il-poteredacquisto-in-lire-ed-euro-con-la-macchina-del-tempo/
14 See: http://contropiede.ilgiornale.it/personaggi-dimenticati-luigi-alleman diluomo-che-si-vendette-forse-per-25-000-lire/
15 'Catania-Avellino: dallo scandalo del '49 ai giorni nostri'; cf. http://avellinocalcio.it/catania-avellino-dallo-scandalo-del-49-ai-giorni-nostri
16 'Il calcioscommesse degli anni Ottanta'; cf. www.ilpost.it/2012/06/04/il-calcioscommesse-degli-anni-ottanta/
17 'Calcio, Roma: Rolex, chiesta archiviazione per Sensi'; cf. http://sport.repubblica.it/news/sport/calcio-roma-rolex-chiesta-archiviazione-per-sensi/41892?refresh_cens
18 'Calciopoli: Carraro prosciolto'; cf. www.napolisport.net/calciopoli-carraro-prosciolto/
19 Cf. http://www.calcioefinanza.it/2016/10/03/demos-calcio-italiano-tifosi/
20 Cf. http://archiviostorico.gazzetta.it/2000/settembre/21/Udinese_sono_tre_passaporti_falsi_ga_0_0009212189.shtml?refresh_ce-cp
21 Cf. www.infodata.ilsole24ore.com/2015/04/14/se-potessi-avere-calcola-il-poteredacquisto-in-lire-ed-euro-con-la-macchina-del-tempo/
22 'Passaporti falsi: patteggiano Recoba e Oriali'; cf. www.gazzetta.it/Calcio/Squadre/Inter/Primo_Piano/2006/05_Maggio/25/patteggia.shtml
23 'Last Bet, tutto lo scandalo è iniziato così nel 2011';cf. http://sport.sky.it/calcio/2013/12/17/calcioscommesse_cronistoria_scheda.html
24 Cf. http://bari.repubblica.it/cronaca/2011/02/10/news/calcio_giovanile_proposta_indecente_tremila_euro_e_perdi_la_partita-12277432/
25 Cf. https://sport.sky.it/calcio/2011/06/01/scommesse_scandalo_testi_intercettazioni.html
26 Ibid.
27 Cf. www.varesesport.com/2015/calcioscommesse-spunta-anche-il-sequestro-di-persona-ulizio-regista-carluccio-esecutore/
28 The DIA is the Italian equivalent to the British National Crime Agency.
29 Excerpt 2 DIA authorised document (2017).
30 Excerpt 4 DIA authorised document (2017).
31 Excerpt 5 DIA authorised document (2017).
32 'La Corte d'Appello conferma la condanna per Codognotto'; cf. http://nuovavenezia.gelocal.it/venezia/cronaca/2014/11/12/news/la-corte-d-appelloconferma-la-condanna-per-codognotto-1.10300917

33 Excerpt 4b interview C (2017).
34 Cf. www.lanotiziagiornale.it/nel-mondo-del-calcio-sporco-affare-e-malaffare-nello-sport-piu-amato-del-pianeta-ecco-la-spectre-internazionale-che-decide-il-destino-dei-giocatori-e-ricicla-i-soldi-del-crimine-con-il-beneplacito-de/
35 Cf. www.osservatoriosport.interno.gov.it/allegati/leggi/Normativa%20italiana/LEGGI/l_n_401_89_come_int_l_%20217_10.pdf
36 Cf. www.transparency.org/country/DEU
37 Cf. www.ilgiornale.it/news/interni/882323.html; Europol, www.europol.europa.eu/newsroom/news/update-results-largest-football-match-fixing-investigation-in-europe
38 Cf. www.termometropolitico.it/1231332_sondaggio-demos-italiano-non-credono-piu-nostro-calcio.html
39 Corradino (ANAC); Excerpt 10 interview C (2017); c.f. (Corradino, 2016).
40 Cf. http://m.stop-match-fixing-italia.org/1/upload/indaginematchfixing_italia.pdf
41 Excerpt 3 interview LSB (2017).
42 Cf. www.prontoprofessionista.it/articoli/3950/giustizia-sportiva/

References

Bourdieu, P. and Passeron, J., 1990. *Reproduction in Education, Society and Culture*. London: Sage.

Corradino, M., 2016. *È normale . . . lo fanno tutti. Storie dal vivo di affaristi, corrotti e corruttori*. Milano: Chiarelettere.

de BLIC, D. and Lemieux, C., 2005. The Scandal as Test: Elements of Pragmatic Sociology. *Politix*, 3(71), pp. 9–38.

Di Ronco, A. and Lavorgna, A., 2015. Fair Play? Not So Much: Corruption in the Italian Football. *Trends in Organized Crime*, 18, pp. 176–195.

Durkheim, E., 1912 translated in 2008. *The Elementary Forms of the Religious Life*. Kent: Dover Publications.

Goffman, E., 1986. *Frame Analysis: An Essay on the Organization of Experience*. Lebanon, NH: Northeastern University Press.

The Guardian-online, 2017-last update, Ángel María Villar resigns from Uefa and Fifa positions after arrest in Spain. Available: www.theguardian.com/football/2017/jul/27/angel-maria-villar-resigns-uefa-fifa-spain [August 8, 2017].

Hill, D., 2013. *The Insider's Guide to Match-Fixing in Football*. Toronto: Anne McDermid & Associates Limited.

The Huffington Post-online, 2017-last update, La bolla del calcio italiano è scoppiata: diritti tv al minimo storico, Tavecchio annulla l'asta. Available: www.

huffingtonpost.it/2017/06/10/la-bolla-del-calcio-italiano-e-scoppiata-diritti-tv-al-minimo-s_a_22135931/ [June 10, 2017].

Il Corriere della Sera-online, 2004-last update, "Se li denunci, i tifosi vengono a casa". Available: www.corriere.it/cronache/12_aprile_04/bari-stellini-esposito_20e1d89a-7e2e-11e1-b61a-22df94744509.shtml?refresh_ce-cp [November 13, 2016].

Il Fatto Quotidiano-online, 2013-last update, Franco Carraro, l'improponibile candidato Pdl in Emilia Romagna. Available: www.ilfattoquotidiano.it/2013/01/23/franco-carraro-limproponibile-candidato-pdl-in-emilia-romagna/477839/ [October 13, 2016].

Il Giornale-online, 2006-last update, Da Allemandi a Rossi, tutti gli scandali del calcio. Available: www.ilgiornale.it/news/allemandi-rossi-tutti-scandali-calcio.html [July 20, 2016].

Il Resto del Carlino-online, 2017-last update, Ravenna calcio, sponsor fittizi e fondi distratti. Quattro imputati per il crac del 2012. Available: www.ilrestodelcarlino.it/ravenna/cronaca/calcio-fallimento-1.3279856 [August 13, 2017].

Il Secolo XIX-online, 2015-last update, Bancarotta fraudolenta e corruzione, condannato il faccendiere Fouzi. Available: www.ilsecoloxix.it/p/genova/2015/03/26/ARY1v0vD-faccendiere_fraudolenta_corruzione.shtml [August 23, 2016].

Il Sole 24 Ore-online, 2017-last update, Calcio, il giro d'affari in Europa cresce ancora e sfiora i 25 miliardi. Available: www.ilsole24ore.com/art/finanza-e-mercati/2017-07-12/calcio-giro-d-affari-europa-cresce-ancora-e-sfiora-25-miliardi-152331.shtml?uuid=AE2LUEwB&refresh_ce=1 [August 14, 2017].

Jacobsson, K. and Lömarck, E., 2008. A Sociology of Scandal and Moral Transgression: The Swedish "Nannygate" Scandal. *Acta Sociologica*, 51(3), pp. 203–216.

Kantola, A. and Vesa, J., 2013. Mediated Scandals as Social Dramas: Transforming the Moral Order in Finland. *Acta Sociologica*, 56(4), pp. 295–308.

La Gazzetta dello Sport-online, 2017-last update, Moggi, respinto il ricorso: la radiazione è definitiva. Available: www.gazzetta.it/Calcio/16-03-2017/moggi-respinto-ricordo-radiazione-definitiva-190111241069.shtml [April 24, 2017].

La Gazzetta dello Sport-online, 2015-last update, Gervasoni: "Ho truccato una dozzina di partite e corrotto 60 calciatori". Available: www.gazzetta.it/Calcio/10-10-2015/gervasoni-ho-truccato-dozzina-partite-corrotto-60-calciatori-calcioscommesse-130454397967.shtml [November 24, 2016].

La Gazzetta dello Sport-online, 2012-last update, Ira Buffon: "Una vergogna la fuga di notizie Ma il calcio attuale mi ha sorpreso". Available: www.gazzetta.it/Europei/2012/30-05-2012/buffon-no-comment-monti-ma-niente-paternali-giornalisti-911385609828.shtml [November 10, 2016].

La Gazzetta dello Sport-online, 2006-last update, Passaporti falsi: patteggiano Recoba e Oriali. Available: www.gazzetta.it/Calcio/Squadre/Inter/Primo_ Piano/2006/05_Maggio/25/patteggia.shtml [October 24, 2015].

La Repubblica-online, 2016-last update, L'ultima curva, gli italiani in fuga dal calcio. Available: www.repubblica.it/sport/calcio/2016/10/02/news/atlante_ tifo_italiani_in_fuga_dal_calcio-148926536/ [July 12, 2017].

La Repubblica-online, 2015-last update, Calciopoli, Cassazione: "Arbitri, tv, designatori: Moggi comandava tutto". Available: www.repubblica.it/sport/calcio/2015/09/09/news/calciopoli_cassazione_moggi_strapotere_ingiustificato_-122527729/ [August 21, 2016].

La Repubblica-online, 2009-last update, Ocse: calcio usato per riciclare denaro sporco Un tentato acquisto di club italiano tra i casi. Available: www.repubblica.it/2009/07/sport/calcio/ocse-calcio/ocse-calcio/ocse-calcio.html [September 12, 2016].

La Stampa-online, 2015-last update, Calciopoli, le tappe dello scandalo. Available: www.lastampa.it/2015/03/23/sport/calcio/qui-juve/calciopoli-letappe-dello-scandalo-N2FeK2vESv7DY1XbqbrMQK/pagina.html [August 24, 2016].

Loland, S. and McNamee, M., 2000. Fair Play and the Ethos of Sports: An Eclectic Philosophical Framework. *Journal of the Philosophy of Sport*, XXVII, 63–80

Ritzer, G. and Stepnisky, J., 2017. *Modern Sociological Theory*. London: Sage.

The Telegraph-online, 2017-last update, Prince William and David Cameron Caught up in Fifa Corruption Scandal. Available: www.telegraph.co.uk/news/2017/06/27/prince-william-david-cameron-caught-fifa-corruption-scandal/ [June 27, 2017].

Turner, V., 1982. *From Ritual to Theatre: The Human Seriousness of Play*. New York: PAJ Publications.

Vignati, A., 2016. *Scandalo Calcio*. Milano: HOW2 Edizioni.

Chapter 4

Hidden power
The 'Calcio' mafia style

> The ['ndrangheta's] quest for [social and political] consensus and for publicity goes also through the control of local soccer. Soccer is a tool; it is a strong form of publicity.
>
> (Gratteri in Huffingtonpost, 2015)[1]

As this quote by Nicola Gratteri – one of the most dedicated Antimafia prosecutors in Italy – underlines, soccer for mafia clans is crucial for maintaining power. However, before attempting to understand and assess how and to what extent the development and the prospering of mafia power is conducive to penetrating corruptive behaviours in soccer practices, it is necessary to re-emphasise what was mentioned in chapter 2, namely the nature of mafia power within national and local boundaries. There is, in fact, in the birth, in the growth and also in the decline of mafia groups a necessary link not only with the physical territory of reference but also with the social, political and human resources of that territory.

Mafia power has been described as a territorial sovereignty (Paoli, 2003, 2007; Lupo, 2011), but this territorial sovereignty is polymorphous, depending on the group and on socio-historical circumstances. For example, territorial sovereignty of mafia groups in Southern Italy has often meant *violent* control of the territory (meant in the physical and geographical sense), thanks to the availability and the employability of weapons and military power. Recently, however, in the investigation and trials for the so-called *Mafia Capitale* case in Rome,[2] both the concept of territory and the concept of control have been questioned: territory, especially in central and Northern Italy, can also refer to institutions, while control can also be achieved through the establishment of relationships with the local system of power in which corruption has become *doxic*.

This chapter has two main objectives. It will first present the dynamics and the manifestations of corruption and mafia power in national soccer and then switch the focus to the three main mafia organisations as presented in the latest investigations, mainly at the local level.

The national networks between mafias and soccer

As mentioned in the previous chapters, when assessing the penetration of mafia interests and money into soccer practices, it is first necessary to make a distinction between traditional/original territories (southern regions of Italy) and non-traditional/derivative ones (central and northern regions). In original territories, investing in soccer supports the building of consensus, in a way similar to other social practices, while it might not be necessarily linked to money-making. This is not the case in the north or the centre of the country, in derivative territories, where mafia clans act as economic syndicates; thus, consensus through soccer is less relevant than the money soccer brings.

In derivative territories, investing in soccer certainly means profit-seeking, but it can also mean the advancement of either economic or political standing of certain individuals. In other words, in traditional territories, investing in soccer means first and foremost investing in the relationship with the local community to gain social consensus. On the other hand, in non-traditional territories, investing in soccer is a means to achieve other goals such as financial benefits or political endorsement, because the relationship with the local communities, at least at first, has not been cemented yet.[3]

Another distinction must be made between low-level and high-level practices and interests. At the low level, mafia interests include endorsements of amateur players from the beginning of their careers. At the high level we find professionals and entrepreneurs, match-fixing and money laundering. In between these two there are many other practices, part of a system where corruption and trafficking of favours are the key and the norm to ensure control of the industry.

As in many other markets where the presence of mafia interests has been ascertained, there is, therefore, the need to first understand the local dynamics when investigating the big scandals. As said earlier in this book, 'scandals' in Italy's soccer world are not uncommon, and they resound in public perception due to the importance of soccer as a national sport.

When approaching national scandals, the complication often lies in differentiating systems of corruptive practices from systems of corruption as manifestations of mafia power. Corruption employed by mafia clans has the essential role of creating consensus, building trust with the power field, which allows mafia clans to prosper in society without creating the social alarm usually associated with their use of violence. This is important for investigative purposes and certainly for evidence gathering and prosecution, but in the public domain, the two phenomena often seem to overlap.

Systems of corruption and mafia systems of corruption in soccer, when they lead to scandals of national resonance, are seen as 'peas of the same pod'. The reasons for this are varied. First and foremost, investigative and judicial operations involving malpractice, crimes and corruption in soccer are often multi-level and complex and have often revealed a system of personal favours that seems very similar to the one employed by mafia groups in the country (DNA, 2016; Pratticò, 2014). Secondly, the economic weight of such scandals is often paired with the social reactions to them, due to the prominent meaning of soccer as a national sport. As noticed by the public prosecutors in Cremona during Operation Last Bet in 2010–2011,[4] commonly known as 'Scommessopoli' or 'Calcio-Scommesse':[5]

> So great are the attention, the enthusiasm and the trust in soccer matches, for their social dimension, and so great are the economic interests around them, that the alteration of matches is perceived, for right or for wrong, as no less important than phenomena of corruption in politics or public administration. It harms, through unfair accumulation of wealth, an enormous number of individuals: not just the state and soccer clubs, but millions of fans who feel disappointed and betrayed.

After this poignant consideration on the impact of soccer scandals at a general level, the public prosecutor continues:[6]

> It is worrying, and it needs attention from a preventative perspective, the fact that these illicit mechanisms are getting clearer and clearer. For example, starting from November 2010, a low-profile soccer match between the Cremonese and the Paganese could attract the attention (and already has) of individuals and groups linked to organised crime. They can invest without risks and multiply their cash capitals. Their stories and the contexts in which they operate are described in the investigations from Cremona to Bari.

The significance of personal contacts and network proximity

With soccer scandals of national resonance, therefore, public indignation – if any – is not necessarily paired with expectations of 'justice' within the criminal justice process. Public prosecutor Guido Salvini stresses this problem:

> [. . .] sport fraud is subjected, at the criminal law level, to a legislation that is outdated (1989) and does not take into consideration the infiltration of organised crime.[7]

As argued in chapter 2, mafia crimes and connections to mafias attract public attention, as the topic of 'mafia' is considered 'sexy' for a number of reasons, linked mostly but not only to American cinema and literature (Sergi, 2017; Dickie, 2013; Allum, 2013). It follows that when the *sexiness* of the mafia topic meets the glamour of high-level soccer games, public attention is even higher. The media resonance of events surrounding the soccer player Giuseppe Sculli are representative of these dynamics while at the same time uncovering the complicated set of relationships between mafia clans, illegal soccer practices, organised groups of fans (Ultras) and corruption.

Giuseppe Sculli, a professional soccer player playing for different Serie A teams (Genoa, Lazio, Juventus, Crotone) and for the national team, has been involved in different scandals since 2006. He is the nephew of a very well-known 'ndrangheta boss, Giuseppe Morabito (known as 'Tiradrittu', arrested in 2004); other members of his family have been at different times charged and/or arrested for involvement with mafia activities as members of the mafia clan. Investigations of him, not always followed by official charges, have involved attempts to influence local political elections, vote fraud through intimidation and violence, murder and drug trafficking.[8] With his problematic kinship and his own personal vicissitudes, Sculli was first involved in a scandal in 2006, when the Disciplinary Commission of the Professional League (Lega Calcio[9]) disqualified him for eight months after judging him responsible for fixing a match between Crotone and Messina in 2002. The Lega Calcio[10] noticed in the first instance that:

> Judging from the content of the conversations between Sculli, Criaco and 'Rocco' [Criaco was at the time a player in the Messina FC and Rocco was identified as the cousin of Sculli] in the days immediately before the match, there seemed to be an agreement between the two societies [they refer to an agreement with the president of the Crotone FC], finalised at favouring Messina.

In this agreement, Sculli seemed to demand higher sums of money and to reject smaller presents. Transcripts of the phone communications intercepted by the prosecutors in Calabria[11] show how "it is always Sculli who reveals his own behaviours"[12] in relation to his performance during the match and the illicit financial gain agreed to and obtained by himself and by others. Sculli was under investigation again during the very famous soccer scandal in 2011 known as 'Calcio-Scommesse' originating from Operation Last Bet[13] from the Procura of Cremona. As mentioned in chapter 3, within this operation, another important set of relationships was unveiled: first, the relationship with the *Ultras*, and second, the relationship with mafia environments. As for the first point in particular, the judge for the preliminary hearing in Cremona[14] assessed the contribution of Giuseppe Sculli to the criminal network involved in high-profile illegal betting and match-fixing practices. The court listed elements of risk that all contributed to the investigations into Sculli's behaviours:

> The employment of individuals active in organised crime groups – such as the Albanian Safet Altic, detained for drug offences [and close to the Fiandaca mafia clan in Sicily]; his relationship with the most extreme part of the 'Ultras' of the Genoa FC – such as Massimo Leopizzi, already involved in match-fixing [. . .]; the relationship between Omar Milanetto [also a soccer player for the Genoa FC] and Altic [they call each other by first name, a sign of routine contact – Sculli as well uses a friendly tone with Altic, calling him "bro" (fraté)]; the use of cryptic language [i.e. saying "documents" instead of "money"]; the involvement of other players in the conduct, such as Milanetto and Kaladze. These profiles of risk all give a sense of continuity of Sculli's behaviours and imply stability in his availability to the criminal network [. . .] to influence matches, through the criminal network, for financial gain.

As for the second point, the networks Sculli could access in Rome were people more or less formally linked to the Mafia Capitale network, whose activities have been uncovered, and under trial, since 2014 within 'Operation Mondo di Mezzo'.[15] Sculli had direct contact with Massimo Carminati, the main character of the Mafia Capitale network, who was convicted with a 20-year sentence in July 2017 on corruption charges[16] – and also connected to the Mancuso 'ndrangheta clan in Calabria. It is difficult, in Rome, to understand the fine line between personal contacts, corruption systems and mafia infiltrations, and the network around Sculli is part of this.

As noticed by Michele Prestipino, one of the leading antimafia prosecutors in the Mafia Capitale investigation, during our interview in Rome in July 2016, "Today corruption is not just about buying an illicit act, it is also about buying a person [. . .] mafia and corruption are not always two linked phenomena, but they can cross paths,"[17] which is why understanding personal networks – in the case of Sculli – is fundamental in both cases of corruption and cases of mafia influence. As explained in chapter two, social capital is crucial to understanding the links and mutual influences among ordinary local power-mafia and soccer fields.

*****

Another example of an implication of a soccer player with mafia business through territorial proximity and personal contacts is the case of the extortion of Marco Biagianti, a player for the Catania F.C., in Sicily, by members of the mafia clan 'Piacenti'. As we read in the conviction sentence published by the Tribunal of Catania in December 2016,[18] Biagianti was in contact with Rosario Piacenti, who was part of a group of fans named simply 'Ultras' and who was following not just the matches but also the training of the team. Together with another fan, Piacenti had attempted to extort €5000 from Biagianti as a contribution to the expenses and pending legal fees of the Ultras, also ensuring the perplexed player that that was a common practice with others in the team. As the investigation unravelled, it became known that another clan in the city were extorting protection fees from other members of the family of Biagianti and their businesses; thus, the prosecutors were attempting to understand whether there was a link. Rosario Piacenti had also already been convicted for extortion and loan-sharking, with the aggravating factor of having used the mafia method as a member of the clan Piacenti. As that was a known fact in the area and across the team members and staff, it was fair to consider that the request for money was more than a simple request for contribution but rather an event of extortion through an implicit and indirect threat originating precisely from the mafia connection. In particular, as the sentence clarifies,[19] the request for a monetary contribution to support pending legal fees:

> hints at the proximity with criminal environments to the events surrounding these criminal environments; this definitely leads to an implicit threat being made and to the reasonable belief that there might be consequences and retaliation should the money not be paid.

In an environment like the city of Catania in general, mafia influence is not only known but perceived as being deeply embedded in the territory, as the player Biagianti himself reveals between the lines in his testimony to the court:[20] "as this is Catania, I did not know how to act", meaning how to refuse to pay without retaliation. As concluded by the tribunal:[21]

> The implicit threat lying in the insinuation of proximity to mafia environments and the request of a certain amount of money, without any real reason for this request, certainly constitute non-equivocal and direct acts aimed at forcing the victim to pay an unjustified sum to the defendants.

What essentially the Tribunal in Catania is saying in this excerpt is that in mafia-dense territories, where the proximity to mafia clans and affiliates is certainly a more frequent event than one might think, this proximity brings with itself an aura of fear, fear of retaliation more specifically because of the perceived omnipresence of mafia influence. The link between organised groups of fans, the threat of violence associated with them, amplifies the risk of mafia clans being involved, if necessary, in this violence, thus enhancing the power of intimidation of any request made by individuals close to the clans and to the Ultras. It is a world – the one where mafia power prospers – where the closer someone feels to mafia members, the more the strength of the intimidating power of the group grows out of fear of this proximity.

*****

Finally, the events surrounding soccer player, former '*azzurro*'[22] member and 2006 World Cup champion Vincenzo Iaquinta, for different reasons, also are representative of how the world of soccer can be absorbed within the mafia influence, even if, like in the previous case, the criminality of the activities related to soccer might not seem that serious. In 2015, investigations relating to the presence of mafia-type activities in the Emilia Romagna region, linked to a mafia clan in Calabria (the clan "Grande-Aracri), led to the arrest of 147 people (Sergi and Lavorgna, 2016). The investigation,[23] named 'Operation Aemilia', did attract considerable attention from the press (as do all cases of mafia activity). Amongst other things, it involved Iaquinta's alleged possession of illegal weapons, and the alleged participation in the affairs of the mafia clan by his father, Giuseppe Iaquinta. Both were charged with having facilitated the activities of the 'ndrangheta clan in Emilia Romagna – a northern Italian region. The prosecutors, in their reconstruction of the criminal networks, presented evidence of both father and son having contact with different members of the clan and participating in summits and reunions both in Calabria and in the north of Italy. The pictures of the meeting at Giuseppe Iaquinta's house with the boss, Nicolino Grandi Aracri, went viral online.[24] The soccer player was seen with his father at dinners in Reggio Emilia and in particular at a dinner on July 5, 2011,[25] during which, according to the prosecutors "relevant matters for the economic development of the clan were discussed".

Considering "the principle of confidentiality, which requires that only associates of the 'ndrangheta participates in these reunions", the position of Vincenzo Iaquinta and his father seemed to complicate things.[26] According to prosecutors, the proximity with a soccer player of Vincenzo Iaquinta's calibre and the possibility to offer marketing products and gadgets linked to him and his matches were sources of status and prestige for certain members of the clan. This proximity was used as leverage to approach other key individuals. While the trial was still ongoing at the end of 2017, problematic new details on the position of Vincenzo Iaquinta still seem to emerge, like for example episodes in which the clan resorted to intimidation to secure the player for certain matches.[27] The impact of the involvement of the soccer player within a mafia environment has obviously attracted the attention of national and international media. With Iaquinta declaring to journalists that he does "not even know what the 'ndrangheta is",[28] and despite the levity of charges against him when compared to the others involved, the media have still considerably focused their coverage of Operation Aemilia, at least at the beginning, around the involvement of the World Cup champion.

Match-fixing, illegal betting, ticket touting: mafia's interests in national soccer

At the national level, aside from the connection of 'famous' individuals from the world of soccer to mafia business, the interests of mafia clans and affiliates have been extremely varied, from the evergreen match-fixing to money laundering and general social capital gain strategies (Di Ronco and Lavorgna, 2015). The two 'fields' – soccer and mafia – meet because of shared interests and mutual benefits; they both contribute to and express corruption as *doxa* in the Italian power field. Soccer is a field where mafia clans can seek to obtain a share of lucrative activities through provision of services. As with the fields of politics and entrepreneurship, the blame cannot be placed only on the 'evil' mafia that corrupts and infects an otherwise clean social space: it is, rather, a web of reciprocal interests which makes it difficult to assign blame.

As we will see at the end of this chapter, all three main Italian mafia syndicates – cosa nostra, 'ndrangheta and camorra – 'play' soccer for mostly the same reasons and with mostly the same objectives, both nationally and locally. In May 2016, the District Antimafia Prosecutors (DDA – hereinafter all the DDA offices will be referred to as 'Antimafia') in Naples arrested 10 people for the fixing of two matches (and two other attempted) in the national Serie B second division during the 2013–2014 championship. Among those arrested were mafia members and four players, one of whom, Armando Izzo, at the time was playing for the Genoa Serie A team first division. Importantly, Izzo is also the nephew of the boss of Secondigliano near Naples[29] – and he is involved in the fraud, echoing the previously mentioned case of Sculli. The four players were under investigation with the charge of 'external participation in mafia affairs'. The case revolved around matches played in Campania, where a camorra clan (Vanella Grassi, from Secondigliano) invested conspicuous sums in the Modena-Avellino and Avellino-Reggina matches. The money was used to corrupt players and fix results, and then bets. The four players under investigations acted as brokers for the mafia boss to influence others and cut the profits for themselves and others. In December 2016, the FIGC (Federazione Italiana Giuoco Calcio, Italian Soccer Federation Authority) deferred to the federal prosecutor eight soccer players, the president of the Avellino Soccer Club, and two clubs, Avellino and Torbellamonaca, for illicit conduct in soccer practice. The disciplinary deferral, with proceedings starting in 2017, is tightly linked with the antimafia investigation and confirms the economic nature of the corrupted practices at the basis of this case.

The FIGC is called to evaluate the position of these players:

> because they conspired to commit a series of disciplinary illicit acts [. . .] for the alteration of the regular course and the result of matches within the second division championship. Their aim was to ensure financial gain by receiving money from individuals belonging to organised crime groups involved in match-fixing and illegal betting. Their plan was executed with a stable arrangement and through distribution and diversification of roles.[30]

As noted by Andrea Abodi, president of the Lega Serie B Second Division league, "even though this case is regarding just two matches two years ago, it is quite serious anyway. Once again, organised crime mixes with soccer despite the efforts to ensure integrity and respect of soccer practices." Clearly the presence of mafia interests in illegal betting and match-fixing increases the profile of the case.

The prosecutor on the case in Naples, Filippo Beatrice, notes: "The system is sick . . . I can say it quite convinced . . . that there is *omertà* and it is even getting worse in the world of soccer when it comes to mafia interests."[31] He adds:

> This is a business interest. It is not an occasional event; we cannot say that entire championships have been compromised, but we can say that in many soccer matches there are individuals who are not just there to play soccer.

Also commenting on this case, a national antimafia prosecutor (who prefers to remain anonymous) reminded us in our interview in Rome in December 2016 that everything is connected in the underworld: "High profits are obviously linked to betting. The more they bet, the more they can increase profits and the more they can reinvest these profits in the drug trade, for example."

Indeed, the interests in soccer, when the national leagues are involved, are unsurprisingly linked with money, mostly through investments in business opportunities but also through the laundering of the proceeds of crime. In 2014, the Judge for Preliminary Investigations (GIP) in Milan within the Antimafia 'Operation Rinnovamento'[32] confirmed the arrest of 59 individuals for mafia and mafia-related offences, such as arms trafficking, corruption, extortion and drug trafficking, all of which were more or less linked to one of the most powerful 'ndrangheta clans in the city of Reggio Calabria, also active in Milan (clan Libri-De Stefano-Tegano). While uncovering a drug trafficking network between Santo Domingo and Bulgaria via Milan, as well as money-laundering activities in Switzerland and investments in Hong Kong and Dubai, the investigation also prevented the 'ndrangheta clan from obtaining the contract for catering services at the San Siro (Meazza) stadium in Milan for 2014 and 2015. The trials in 2015 and 2016 largely confirmed the mafia interests in the subcontracts for the management of the stadium. However, the central figure of the investigation, an entrepreneur charged with external participation in mafia business, Cristiano Sala, was acquitted in 2016 of this charge, while still convicted (2 years and 6 months imprisonment) for corruption of a *carabiniere*[33] named Carlo Milesi (bought with only €1000) for the catering contract of the stadium. This story goes far beyond soccer and mafia interests. It demonstrates the penetrating reach of mafia power and the mafia methods – *doxa* – into professional soccer, where money and business rule strategic networks. From the court files it can be seen how mafia clans had multiple interests at play, which converged with entrepreneurial opportunities they were able to pursue.

The interactions between Cristiano Sala and 'ndrangheta key figures (especially the arrested and convicted boss Giuseppe Pensabene) around Milan have been monitored and intercepted on different occasions. Sala was both a victim and an offender. In fact, Sala's bankrupt financial activities had brought him to owe money to some creditors (the Martino brothers, also linked to the clans in Calabria). He then decided to ask for a loan from the Pensabene clan (which they gave, subject to extremely high interest – +20% interest rate *monthly* or 50% every *six months* against a +11.62% national *annual* rate).[34] He struggled with the payments for a couple of years in 2012 and 2013, and the boss, Pensabene, used his reputation in the 'ndrangheta clan to intimidate him. Towards the end of 2013, Sala turned into an offender himself through corruption of a law enforcement agent to make sure that his catering business could win the tender at the San Siro Stadium. This was his attempt to both increase profits through legal activity and to ingratiate the clans by offering them a share of his activity in lieu of some of the missing or delayed payments. By paying the *carabiniere* (Carlo Milesi) to falsely declare that his competitor was hiring irregular workers and also spread the false news to the media, Cristiano Sala attempted to have the competitor excluded from the tender. This is one of the typical mafia *doxa*, in this case 'learned' and 'borrowed' by Sala. However, as his conversations with Milesi were wiretapped, the plan did not work. From the intercepted communications, we see how the plan was supposed to be carried out through the same intimidation method used by the mafia clan.[35]

MILESI: We have talked with the person who has signed the contract for Milan Entertainment [the competitor].
SALA: Wow, Cefaliello. He sits on the board of Fininvest next to Marina Berlusconi[36]!
MILESI: Yes, he does and he is also counsellor for A.C. Milan . . .
SALA: Sure, the group . . . but did you scare him?
MILESI: Well! We . . . he understood . . . we sent the documents, to him directly . . . then we talked to [others . . .] Anyway we will strike big . . . tomorrow we deposit the documents [falsified documents attesting that the competitor is hiring irregular workers] to the police.
SALA: Ha, yes!
MILESI: And then . . . and then! Then the press will give the news!
SALA: Well done! Bravo!

This set of events, which has obviously been of interest to the Italian media and general public, is indeed a clear example of how mafia interests and power manipulate and turn their luck around through the use of classic methods of intimidation and extortion, or by having others, outsiders, use them too, while investing in traditional organised crime businesses such as the drug trade. Victims of mafia extortion might become external actors in the expansion of mafia power, willingly or unwillingly, directly or indirectly. Crucially, mafia groups might not necessarily and strategically direct their interest towards a certain industry or business such as professional soccer; their infiltration can be opportunistic and dependent on a tangled web of victimisation through intimidation, extortion and exercise of power that comes with the availability of cash.

The typology of contacts that different mafia clans can have with the world of soccer at the national level is, as mentioned, very composite and is manifested through different, more or less deviant or delinquent, conduct. For example, relationships between members of the clan and Ultras of Juventus F.C. have been monitored in different investigations. As noticed by Marco Di Lello, president of the Mafia & Sport Committee within the Antimafia Commission in Rome,[37] "Even though, at the moment, the Juventus society is not involved either as a victim or as a conspirator in the offences, there is a grey zone around them that we need to investigate." In particular, these declarations arrived at a moment, in late 2016, in which the antimafia prosecutors in Torino made public their investigations on the alleged infiltration of 'ndrangheta interests in ticket touting for Juventus's matches, the most profitable, as they are the most titled of Italian soccer clubs, first in the Lega Serie A (first division).

During operation 'Alto Piemonte'[38] – in the second half of 2016 and early 2017 – the prosecutors evidenced the theory that managers of the soccer club provided the tickets to (alleged) affiliates from the Pesce-Bellocco clan in exchange for control of the various Ultras groups in the stadium. The investigation uncovered various criminal activities such as extortion, arson, kidnapping, illicit investments in the night-time economy, vandalism and even attempted murder, alongside the attempt to run the ticket touting of the soccer club. According to the investigation files, a member of the Dominiello family linked to the Pesce-Bellocco clan in Rosarno, Calabria, managed to contact managers of the soccer club (who denied their involvement and their knowledge later on to the prosecutors) thanks to the association with a former ultra, Fabio Germani, also founder of the NGO 'Bianconeri d'Italia'. Germani was later acquitted of the charge of external participation in mafia affairs. Saverio Dominiello and his father, Rocco, had formed the Ultras group known as 'I Gobbi' which first appeared at the stadium in spring 2013. According to the prosecutors in Torino, through this group and their contacts with other Ultras, the Pesce-Bellocco clan was seeking to establish contacts with the managers of the soccer club.

Ultimately, it was maintained that the Dominiellos acted as brokers for the mafia group, promising order in the stadium among the Ultras and the other fans in exchange for tickets to sell for higher prices. Father and son have been convicted on charges of mafia association. According to the antimafia prosecutors' documents on the case:[39]

> The ultras used to negotiate to have part of the tickets directly from the soccer club, thanks to their leader. The 'ndrangheta clan participated in the business by offering control and protection of the different ultras groups.

The antimafia prosecutors transferred the relevant documents to the FIGC, which can examine the allegations for a disciplinary hearing.[40] The case, at the beginning of 2018, is at the appeal trial, and the Mafia & Sport Committee of the Parliamentary Antimafia Commission has been carrying out its auditions across various soccer clubs in the country. The interception and recording of conversations made by the authorities working on the investigation 'Alto Piemonte' are nevertheless a cause for concern. First of all, they indicate how Saverio Dominiello did indeed seem to have a prominent role and reputation among fans and Ultras. He said to Alessandro D'Angelo, security manager, on June 7, 2013:[41] "Now they are scared of me [. . .] can I ask him [one of the Juventus managers] to do it differently this year and not like last year?"

D'Angelo reassures him: "I want you to feel OK, as we are OK, we are in this together." Both the soccer club and the lawyers of Dominiello have been denying the strategic involvement of 'ndrangheta interests in the business of ticket touting, and obviously any criminal wrongdoing will be judged in a court of law. However, during an interception on April 14, 2014, of Saverio Dominiello and members of the Pesce-Bellocco clan in Rosarno, Dominiello said "We go forward! We have everyone's agreement and no one can ask 'what have you done?'. . . We go forward and we might even get the whole stand of the stadium!", thus giving cause for concern about mafia interests in this case.

With the criminal appeal trial still ongoing, the FGCI has disqualified and fined in the first degree of the proceedings Juventus president Andrea Agnelli for negligence, D'Angelo (former security manager of the Juventus), Calvo (former commercial director of the Juventus) and Merulla (head of the ticket office of the club). However, the existence of such a 'grey area' in soccer should be a concern in itself. As noticed by the president of the Mafia & Sport Committee within the Parliamentary Antimafia Commission, Di Lello, Juventus can be considered a 'national patrimony', as it is repeatedly first team in the Serie A (first division) and has an extremely international profile. The reputation of the president Agnelli has already received an extremely powerful blow because of these events, independently to how the sport trial ends.[42] The fact that there are muddy relationships between managers of the club and Ultras or even affiliates of mafia clans, for illicit purposes, appeals at the very least to managerial or even moral responsibilities of the whole soccer industry.

Soccer and the three Italian mafias

The relationships between the field of soccer and the field of mafia and their interests at the national level are necessarily linked to the money soccer generates at high levels and the opportunities money-making offers to anyone, mafiosi included. It is not surprising, in fact, that recently we find that the 'ndrangheta clans are the most involved in soccer, considering their reach into local, national and international markets and their ability to establish strategic social networks at all levels for profit and power.

Before proceeding to an analytical outlook on the intersections between soccer and the local presence of mafia clans – and especially on our detailed case study of Operation Dirty Soccer – it is helpful to look at each of the three mafia associations in Italy, cosa nostra, camorra and 'ndrangheta, in order to briefly pinpoint recent developments from investigative and judicial sources in relation to their involvement with the Italian soccer industry. As argued in chapter 2, it is important to remember that these three mafia associations are not homogeneous – they are all made of various clans with different activities; together, though, they constitute what we have identified in chapter 2 as the Bourdieuian concept of 'field'. Crucially, they are geographically identifiable and identified in their places of origin in the three regions of Sicily, Campania and Calabria, but all of them have projections elsewhere in the country (and abroad).

Cosa nostra – Sicily

Although considerably weakened since their golden age (1970–1990), the clans of the Sicilian mafia have not lost their appetite for either local power or money. Certainly, the local dimension of the clans' involvement with the world of soccer is undeniable and has to do with the normality of relationships between mafia power and their territories. In this sense, the fact that in 2008,[43] in the municipality of Bagheria, near Palermo, a unanimous proposal – then opposed by the mayor – was passed by the town council to name the local stadium after the brother of a mafia boss – has to do more with the intertwining of local relationships than with mafia power over soccer.

Fundamentally, in addition to issues related to accruing symbolic capital such as prestige and status to establish control in rural areas, the relationships between mafia and soccer in Sicily become interesting when looking at its major cities of Palermo and Catania. For one thing, and unsurprisingly, the affair between cosa nostra clans and soccer has been linked to the Palermo soccer club. Various presidents of the soccer club have been investigated because of their (alleged or proved) links with the clans for purposes of profit. Also, the intimidation of mafia groups has been used to solve issues within the club. This was the case in 1997, when president Liborio Polizzi was arrested and charged with external participation in mafia affairs because of a number of activities supporting the clans. Among other things, the prosecutors noticed how he used his connections in the underworld to solve problems within the Palermo soccer club. Protection from cosa nostra means increased ease in doing business and, more importantly, insurance of lack of conflict. With cases such as that of a former player, Fabrizio Miccoli, involved in mafia-style extortion (sentenced to 3.5 years in October 2017),[44] the Palermo soccer club is often at the centre of constant scrutiny over its management, with or without mafia involvement. For example, in July 2017, investigations from the Fiscal Police brought new suspicions of money laundering and corruption against former President Maurizio Zamparini,[45] who has on various occasions been questioned for his denial of any knowledge about the interests of mafia syndicates in Palermo over the soccer team in spite of ongoing and historical investigations.

In Catania, too, the prosecutors have been investigating corruption, mafia and soccer on different occasions – the links between organised groups of fans (Ultras), mafia power and profit-seeking activities have always been under the scrutiny of antimafia prosecutors. For example, in a sentence published by the Tribunal of Catania in October 2014[46] we read that the 13 defendants were charged with participation in an organised crime group (simple, not mafia-type this time) as they constituted an organised group of fans, Ultras, for the Catania FC named A.N.R. (Associazione Non Riconosciuta – Association Not Recognised), engaged in violent and offensive acts against the police and security agents during soccer matches, also thanks to the possession of weapons and explosives. The difficulty of the tribunal here is to draw the line between the organised group of fans and the organised crime group, attempting to understand when the former becomes the latter. The Tribunal says that, while Ultras groups are not equated to organised crime groups by default, the existence of an indeterminate plan of violence makes the Ultras group an organised crime group:[47]

> The excesses of soccer fans – that obviously characterise all the members of this group (the A.N.R.) – are not criminally relevant, they are neutral in a criminal trial. We cannot automatically absorb these excesses within the elements that constitute and prove the existence of an indeterminate plan of violence. When actions manifest in the context of an organised group of fans, we cannot assume that these actions are justified by a predisposition to violence and to commit acts of violence as a group that simply characterises these groups. We cannot, however, say either that belonging to a 'ultras' group is an excuse, a justification for committing acts of violence as if these group exist to have an indeterminate plan of violence in their constitution. When this plan is in existence, then the group is an organised crime group within article 416 of the Criminal Code.

Within this framework, and within the environment of the city of Catania and its mafia dense underworld, it becomes quite clear that any organised crime structure prone to violence becomes a target, also in terms of possible cooperation, of mafia clans. As mafia clans are themselves prone to violence through 'soldier' groups, the connection with organised groups of fans and violent Ultras becomes the obvious choice and benefits both sides. The Ultras can count on the protection and the reputation of mafia clans together with their power of intimidation – often implicit, as seen earlier in the case of Biagianti. Mafia clans gain control of the stadium, and with that come financial opportunities (for example ticket touting or extortion) or further contacts within the soccer club. In these liaisons, both parties seem to win and benefit from each other's sphere of influence, both against the supposed fairness of the game of soccer.

More recently, the events surrounding 'Operation i Treni del Gol'[48] (trains of goals), also by the prosecutors in Catania, are an interesting instance of existing systems of corruption serving and appealing to a range of interests of clans belonging to cosa nostra, extending into Catania's world of local soccer and within the previously mentioned environment of Ultras groups. This investigation is divided into two main sections. The first part in 2015 uncovered an unlawful organisation focusing on soccer fraud involving, among others, the former president of Catania FC, as well as managers, coaches and players in and out of Sicily. The charges tackled the systematic corruption (match-fixing) influencing at least six matches of the Lega Serie B championship in the season 2014/2015. The conspiracy was stable and organised; the president of Catania FC (Antonino Pulvirenti) argued how he "will win the Serie B championship" as he has "learned how it works".[49] The FIGC, which in 2015 judged the case separately from the criminal courts, does not leave any room for doubt:[50]

> It is precisely the cryptic language used which appears symptomatic of behaviours of organised crime, of that 'world in between' that should never have penetrated and contaminated the sport environment, which – we need to repeat it – is based precisely on values of fairness and honesty. We need to observe with regret that, despite the cyclical occurrences of illicit behaviours in sport, never before has the system appeared so vulnerable. Without the intervention of the criminal justice system, sport regulations alone would be inadequate to repress, or prevent, criminal behaviours of such intensity.

While the system of corruption behind the championship shook fans and worried sport authorities, the second part of the same operation, since 2016, led to more arrests and involved individuals with proven links with one of the main clans of the city, the notorious Santapaola clan. According to prosecutors, the cosa nostra clan has been attracted to the business of match-fixing and illegal betting primarily as a way to launder money. It is not surprising to find one of the main clans of the city of Catania involved in the vicissitudes of the soccer club, especially considering the general status of mafia clans in the city. As noticed by the National Antimafia Prosecutors (DNA, 2016, p. 66):

> The Santapaola-Ercolano clan [. . .] will want to affirm their prestige both with competitors and with those within cosa nostra in Palermo who want to establish in Catania a new 'family' more aligned to their own strategies. There is no doubt that, on the military and economic levels, and in terms of presence on the territory, other families might have superior potential, but surely these don't enjoy the favours of Palermo and they do not have a genetic mafia code as the Santapaolas do.

Accessing and controlling activities like soccer, for laundering purposes as well as for exploring new avenues of power and territorial consensus and control, is fundamental in order to assert mafia prestige, especially in a competitive urban environment like Catania. The penetration of mafia power into the activities of the Ultras and/or the management of the Catania soccer club is always under scrutiny. As noticed by Antimafia Prosecutor Alessandro Sorrentino, during his audition by the Antimafia Commission in early 2017,[51] where he was discussing the results of the operation and trial against an organised group of Ultras (named A.N.R. – Associazione Non Riconosciuta – 'Association Not Recognised') in Catania described earlier:[52]

> Even though no direct and explicit contacts with mafia families in the territory have emerged, some of the elements we had – such as internal funding available to members of the groups and possession of drugs or weapons on behalf of others – led us to believe that these

groups (Ultras) were indeed linked to mafia clans, or somehow they represented mafia interests indirectly. [...] Some of the ultras leaders confirmed direct links with mafia clans, either family links or links via previous criminal partnerships [...] these links, even without the explicit use of the mafia name, can lead to mafia interests conditioning management choices in the soccer club and/or mafia intimidation of administrators or others in the soccer club.

Camorra – Campania

In Campania, as in Sicily and in Calabria, the interests of mafia clans range from instrumental and strategic 'friendships' with players or managers of soccer clubs, through match-fixing at both local and national level, to the acquisition of, and infiltration at different levels in, local teams. Various investigations have confirmed how the camorra clans, notoriously concerned with maintaining a pervasive control of their territory, will attempt control over soccer matches or interference with soccer clubs and, if unsuccessful, management of organised groups of fans. Various clans, such as the Mallardo clan from Giugliano (Naples), the D'Alessandro/Di Martino clan from Castellammare di Stabia (Naples), the Licciardi Clan from Masseria Cardone di Napoli and the Misso clan from the Rione Sanità in Naples, are involved in match-fixing and illegal betting via a number of both offline and online methods. It is no surprise to find a variety of different approaches to the soccer industry from different clans, as the camorra clans are many and diversified. For example, Operation Arcobaleno by the DDA in Naples in 2010 has led to the confiscation of shares of the 'Giugliano Calcio', a C2 league team. The Mallardo clan used the soccer club as a front to impose sponsorship and advertisement deals on local traders. Furthermore, the Casalesi clan – one of the most connected, wealthiest and far-reaching criminal organisations in Italy – was involved in 2008 in an attempt to buy a historical Lega Serie A (first division) team, SS Lazio, to reinvest proceeds of crime. 'Operation Broken Wings' – led by the anti-mafia prosecutors in Rome – also led to a charge of stock manipulation for Giorgio Chinaglia, former captain of SS Lazio, who won the 'scudetto' in the 1974–75 season and was considered in the USA – where he played – as "one of Europe's greatest and most charismatic goal scorers".[53] According to the prosecutors, he would act as a dealmaker, a broker, between the clans and business associates in Rome.

The events surrounding the town of Pagani and the Paganese Calcio are particularly representative of how mafia interests are tightly linked with the local politics and economy, as well as how soccer is part of a much larger mechanism of bonding with, and corrupting, the territory.

Operation 'Linea d'ombra'[54] in 2011 was an investigation into a system of favours between politics, business and soccer in Pagani, Campania, and is a clear example of what we termed 'superimposition' of mafia on the local ordinary power field via corruption. The arrests of the former mayor, Alberico Gambino,[55] various managers, entrepreneurs such as Francesco Marrazzo, the president of the Paganese Calcio, Raffaele Trapani, and also affiliates of the camorra-type clan Fezza-D'Auria Petrosino, all resulted from the investigation. According to antimafia prosecutors in Salerno, a criminal system was operational in Pagani in which a trafficking of favours among local politicians and entrepreneurs supported mafia infiltration and subsequent control over public and private activities. With charges ranging from corruption to vote exchange, all aggravated by the use of the mafia method of intimidation and *omertà*, the administration of Pagani was dissolved for mafia infiltration in 2012. At the centre of this system were the activities of the former mayor, Gambino, who, in agreement with his supporter and president of the Paganese Calcio, Raffaele Trapani, had found sponsors for the team when it got promoted to the then-Lega Serie C (now Lega Pro, third division) in mid-2000. While asking for money and sponsoring activities for the Paganese, he also imposed his own hiring decisions or advanced other requests to the businesses involved. Through his political reputation and the criminal support of the mafia clan behind him in case someone refused, this system of forced sponsoring through intimidation and corruption lasted for years and effectively impacted the funding of the Paganese Calcio until the arrests and trial.

In this case, mafia activities were seemingly subordinated to the political agenda, and the soccer world welcomed the mafia's involvement to ensure the system worked. Another manifestation of mafia power in local soccer is linked to the active and primary engagement of the clans in the soccer industry.

The case of the Mondragonese, a Lega Serie D (amateur league) team in the town of Mondragone, known as the town of the notorious camorra-type clan 'La Torre', became well known. In the mid-1990s, Donato (nicknamed Renato) Pagliuca, a former soccer player, was the president of the team, but he was also acting as lieutenant for the camorra boss Augusto La Torre, who was at the time in jail. When Pagliuca was killed in 1995, as also narrated by journalistic reconstructions (Cantona and Di Feo, 2012), he was clashing with the clan because he was focusing too much on the soccer club to establish his leadership in town. Instead of exploiting the soccer team to increase profits for the clan, Pagliuca was using the reputation of the clan to build a stronger team. During his time as manager of the soccer club, the club prospered, and that gave him the social consensus and support he needed to access politicians and businesses and demand contributions and sponsorships for the team. As noted (Cantona and Di Feo, 2012), all contributions and sponsorships were probably perceived as benefitting the Mondragonese club rather than the La Torre clan. The line between the personal criminal and reputational agenda of Pagliuca and the use of mafia methods and social capital (also through soccer) is in this case a really fine one. These cases have in common the power of the mafia method, the strength of local social networks and the leverage of reputation to advance criminal activities, where soccer becomes an instrument or a segment of a larger strategy.

'Ndrangheta – Calabria

All our research, and the latest reports from the national antimafia prosecutors (DNA, 2016), indicate that in the past 20 years the Calabrian 'ndrangheta has been the most actively involved in all different aspects of Italian economy, including soccer. We have seen already in this chapter how recent police investigations have touched upon concerning investments beyond Calabria and in national soccer.

Another example of these investments beyond Calabria comes from investigation in Torino, in the Piemonte region. During an operation led by the antimafia prosecutors in late 2000,[56] the authorities revealed that a local 'ndrangheta clan had lucrative interests in business activities on the territories. Among the clan's business ventures the authorities revealed control of tenders and contracts related to maintenance work in the stadium – specifically for rebuilding the stands and renewal of the seating plan. Because of the urgency of the work, normal tender procedures were suspended. The contracts were therefore assigned through a direct invitation to tender (thus not public) extended to only five companies. It became clear from the investigations that one of the companies was a front to the clan's activities of illegal waste trafficking and that there had been attempts to discourage the competitors (by having other companies bid much lower than they normally would). In this case it was clear that the investments in relation to the soccer industry and in particular into the soccer field was just one among the many other business opportunities that the 'ndrangheta clan could have sought. Albeit soccer here is just another business, this case shows the capacity of penetration of the 'ndrangheta clans in diverse business ventures beyond Calabria, for both legal and illegal means.

Finally, in the last sections of the chapter we will look mostly at some of the local manifestations of the relationship between the Calabrian clans and soccer before moving to the story on Operation Dirty Soccer. In addition to the influence in national soccer, the interests of the clans in soccer are firmly linked to the local territories. In some cases, from interference in local teams, there are effects on the national championship as well, with scandals in the media questioning the reputation of a team before any trial has finished. This is the case for Crotone FC, in the 2016–2017 Premier League, whose management has been under scrutiny since 2008, with 'Operation Puma' led by the antimafia prosecutors in Catanzaro. On that occasion, which ended with no convictions, the prosecutors argued that Raffaele Vrenna, president of Crotone FC, and his brother, Giovanni, an entrepreneur, together with former magistrate Francesco Tricoli, had acted to evade taxes and confiscation by fictitiously registering assets in other people's names, thus shifting ownership.

Moreover, in November 2016 – while the team was playing in Lega Serie A – the Court of Appeal rejected the prosecutors' theory and provided for the soccer team not to be confiscated, as the prosecutors had asked. The court, in this case, did not find any connection between the mafia clan Vrenna-Corigliano-Bonaventura and the assets of the Vrenna brothers (despite their shared surname), which instead were found to be legitimate. Regardless of the trial's results, media and fans were looking at the events surrounding the Crotone team with concern, another sign of how media scandals in soccer are indeed perceived as preliminary – at times much more punitive – trials.

As said, however, in the case of the 'ndrangheta clans, the symbiotic relationship with the Calabrian territory and culture and the composition of the networks (blood and endogamy) that form, support and hide the clans are fundamental to guarantee their deep penetration into every social and economic activity in the region, including soccer. This is why media scandals suggesting mafia infiltration in the legal economy of the area are easily perceived as the truth before any trial has confirmed the actual involvement. The success of the clans globally or nationally is very much linked to their presence and their penetration of the local networks of Calabria. This is why soccer, as a practice of social aggregation in Calabrian communities, can be an essential tool to solidify the bonds with the territory, not only for consensus but also for social control and reinforcement of 'ndrangheta reputation and status.

To exemplify the relationship between 'ndrangheta clans and soccer, we can note how on more than one occasion local soccer clubs in Calabria, or in other parts of Italy but with links to 'ndrangheta, clans in Calabria, have been confiscated as mafia assets. This was the case, for example, for the Rosarnese (Rosarno, Calabria), the Interpiana (Cittanova, Calabria) and the Sapri Calcio (Sapri, Campania). In particular, these three teams have in common the same clan, the Pesce clan from the area of Rosarno – one of the wealthiest and most powerful clans in Calabria. The confirmation that A.C. Rosarno ('Rosarnese') was a family business came during Operations All Clean[57] and All Inside,[58] which in 2011 brought a series of proceedings against the clan. Giuseppina Pesce, the prosecutors' witness and daughter of the boss in the clan of the same name, corroborated the hypothesis of the antimafia prosecutors on how various members of her family had been involved in the management of the team, at times as players, too, across the years. Marcello Pesce, for example, was both manager of the ASD Rosarno Calcio as well as of the Sapri Calcio in 2005, and both teams were confiscated in 2011 (Romani, 2012). It is not unusual for a soccer team to be confiscated in Calabria. One of the latest cases involves the Ferrentino-Chindamo and Lamara clans in Laureana di Borrello (near Reggio Calabria) at the centre of 'Operation Lex', which, in November 2016, led to the confiscation of the Polisportiva Laureanese club, which was fighting for promotion to a higher league.

Furthermore, in 2011, antimafia prosecutors requested the confiscation of the Interpiana soccer club in Cittanova, which together with the Sapri Calcio played in the Serie D (amateur league) and which was Francesco Pesce's new investment after shadowing the management of ASD Rosarno Calcio. The court order[59] of the Tribunal in Reggio Calabria stated that the two teams (Interpiana and ASD Rosarno Calcio) were like "Mafia-infiltrated businesses where the economic and/or technical management is – or could be – left to 'clean' individuals, while the strategic choices are made in agreement with the mafioso or directly by him". Also, the antimafia prosecutors continued, "The mafioso [mafia clan member] has a fundamental role in the direction and/or sharing of control over the business, independent of his actual shares in the company or from the role he officially holds."

In the interceptions of 'Operation All Inside' we read how soccer is indeed a crucial element to maintain the social standing of the clan Pesce in the territory. This is done, for example, by ensuring that individuals without a criminal record become the owners or managers of mafia-owned business ventures, among which are soccer clubs. Also, forging links with people who might lead to further business opportunities is a classic strategy. For example, says the boss Antonino Pesce, talking about the successes of his son Francesco with an associate:[60]

> He [Francesco] has friends in soccer . . . and they bring business. . . . This is the kind of work you need to do. He [Francesco] managed to get in the system [. . .] in the soccer field . . . you see, there are twenty-two players and they bring money . . . someone arrives from here, someone else from there [. . .] they bring new things. This is the meaning . . . everything, each public space, each conversation . . . better to work in plain sight, avoid the criminal code.

Soccer, therefore, is, for the Pesce clan of the 'ndrangheta in Reggio Calabria, a way to be strongly present in the local social space, a tool to establish new partnerships with the local ordinary power field and a way to diversify their criminal portfolio, possibly by cleaning up the image and the money of the clan. By establishing tight networks with the composite world of interests gravitating around soccer at the local level, the clan can prosper by doing what mafias do best – control the territory. Indeed, the 'ndrangheta clans, as the case of Operation Dirty Soccer also will show in the next chapter, have been particularly successful at exercising forms of diffuse control and at using that control to build their reputation.

Conclusion

Before moving to the case study, we can draw some conclusions about the diversified ways in which mafias and soccer connect at the national and local levels. In particular, we can identify three main levels of contact, making it clear that in order for the macro level corruption mechanisms to become visible, an understanding of the other levels must come first.

- At the *micro* level, the local level, mafia clans have interests in a number of aspects pertaining to the world of soccer. These include, for example, the interference with youth soccer associations – i.e. with young players who are sponsored by a mafia contact and therefore are given more chances in their career against those who are not sponsored, or with the actual sponsoring of youth associations. At the micro, local, level we also find investments from mafia clans in soccer clubs, as previously mentioned, either by buying the club directly or by sponsoring some of the services that help run it. Ticket touting is also part of the range of activities in which groups might be interested in, often thanks to the support of Ultras. The usual range of racket activities, extortions and intimidation linked to mafia presence and reputation comes into play at this level. The micro level is generally, though not exclusively, characterised by activities that enrich the reputation and social prestige of mafias – social prestige

that is a necessary capital for any further activities the clans might embark upon.
- At the *meso* level, which is the level that connects the micro (local) and the macro (national), we find those activities that are rooted in the local environment and feed mafia power and the clans' prestige but also represent springboards for business opportunities and money accumulation that go beyond the local. At this level we find for example the liaisons with Ultras groups that not only amplify the capacity of control of certain territories for the clans but might also open doors for accessing the management of the team – especially when the team plays in the national leagues – or the services linked to that. Also at this level, we can qualify match-fixing and corruption, loosely defined, and the attempts to use personal and local contacts and networks to approach specific players whose behaviours on the pitch might influence the results of a team at the national level. The meso level is distinguished because the more a clan can forge and exploit links in their environments, the more their interests in the local soccer industry have the potential to escalate and reach the national.
- At the *macro* level, in continuation of, but also different from, the meso level, mafia interests become extremely hidden behind a tight network of corporate interests, political collusion and white-collar criminality. This is the level where match-fixing reaches the highest manifestations and touches the winning teams of the league, or where the conditioning of the matches is organised at extremely worrying scales. This is the level where mafia affiliates or external supporters use soccer to access certain elitarian circles of politicians and entrepreneurs, where money is laundered through corporate investments and national or international sponsorships of players, teams and their management. At the macro level, we find the mafias become less visible in terms of actual members and affiliates being directly involved in the activities. We find here instead the *in-betweeners*, individuals close to the interests of the clans but holding power positions in financial or political institutions, thus feeding into a grey area of corruption where different actors from the upperworld and the underworld seem to converge in the field of soccer in Italy.

Hidden power 111

Notes

1 Cf. www.huffingtonpost.it/2015/05/19/calcioscommesse-gratteri-ndrangheta_n_7312462.html
2 Operazione Mondo di Mezzo, procura di Roma – Proc. Pen. No. 30456/10 R.G.N.R. DDA. The operation is known as Mafia Capitale because it was led by the Antimafia Prosecutors in Rome, who charged some of the main players, among which were former terrorist Massimo Carminati and his associate Salvatore Buzzi, with the mafia association charge. The first-degree trial ended in July 2017 and did not confirm the mafia charge; however, severe sentences of corruption in politics and public administration were imposed on the defendants – Cf. www.ft.com/content/4cf9b6de-6d5f-11e7-bfeb-33fe0c5b7eaa
3 Cf. Transcrime, 2015. From Illegal Markets to Legitimate Businesses: The Portfolio of Organised Crime in Europe. In: Commission, E (ed.). *Organised Crime Portfolio*. Available: www.transcrime.it/wpcontent/uploads/2015/03/OCP_Executive-Summary.pdf; see also Varese, F., 2011. *Mafias on the Move: How Organized Crime Conquers New Territories*. Princeton, NJ; Oxford: Princeton University Press, and Varese, F., 2005. *How Mafias Migrate: The Case of the 'Ndrangheta in Northern Italy*. Oxford: University of Oxford.
4 Tribunale Ordinario di Cremona, Ufficio del Giudice per le indagini preliminari Dr Guido Salvini, No. 3628/10 RGNR, no. 827/11 RG GIP – Ordinanza di applicazione delle misure della custodia cautelare in carcere, degli arresti domiciliari e della presentazione all'autorita' di polizia giudiziaria – pp. 16–17.
5 Cf. chapter 3.
6 Tribunale Ordinario di Cremona, Ufficio del Giudice per le indagini preliminari Dr Guido Salvini, No. 3628/10 RGNR, no. 827/11 RG GIP – Ordinanza di applicazione delle misure della custodia cautelare in carcere, degli arresti domicialiari e della presentazione all'autorita' di polizia giudiziaria – pp. 16–17.
7 Ibid.
8 Commissione Parlamentare d'Inchiesta sul fenomeno della criminalità organizzata mafiosa o similare, XIV Legislatura, Doc. XXIII no. 16-bis, Relazione conclusiva di minoranza, 20.01.2006, Relatore Onorevole Lumia, p. 247.
9 In 2010, the Lega Calcio ceased to exist, and it was split into Lega Serie A (premiere division) and Lega Serie B (second division).
10 The Lega Nazionale Professionisti (Italian for *National League of Professionals*), commonly known as Lega Calcio (*Soccer League*), was the governing body that ran the two highest soccer divisions in Italy, namely Serie A and Serie B, from 1946 to 2010. Lega Nazionale Professionisti – Comunicato Ufficiale N. 136 del 28 novembre 2006, pp. 136/495, for download Cf. www.legaseriea.it/

uploads/default/attachments/comunicati/comunicati_m/6767/files/allegati/6772/cu1362345.pdf
11 Procura di Reggio Calabria, Proc. Pen. No. 1691/02 RGNR.
12 Lega Nazionale Professionisti – Comunicato Ufficiale N. 136 DEL 28 novembre 2006, pp. 136/508.
13 Operazione Last Bet, N. 3628/10 R.G.N.R Procura della Repubblica in Cremona.
14 Tribunale Ordinario di Cremona – Ufficio del Giudice per le indagini preliminari Dr. Guido Salvini – Ordinanza di Applicazione delle Misure della Custodia Cautelare in Carcere, degli Arresti Domiciliari e della Presentazione all'Autorita' di Polizia Giudiziaria, N. 3628/10 R.G.N.R. & No. 827/11 R.G.GIP, p. 22.
15 Operazione Mondo di Mezzo, Procura di Roma – Proc. Pen. No. 30456/10 R.G.N.R. DDA.
16 'Massimo Carminati given 20 years for corruption'; cf. www.thetimes.co.uk/article/massimo-carminati-given-20-years-for-corruption-fbjzgmvg5
17 Interview in Rome, Direzione Distrettuale Antimafia, July 2016.
18 Tribunale Penale di Catania, Sez II composizione collegiale, Sentenza del 7 Dicembre 2016, No. 6025/16, RGNR No.14077/12.
19 Ibid., pp. 8–9.
20 Ibid., pp. 9.
21 Ibid., pp. 10.
22 *Azzurro* or '*azzurri*' (plural) refers to players of the Italian soccer team, so named for their light blue shirts.
23 Operazione Aemilia, Procedimento Penale n. 8846/2015/10 R.N.R./Mod. 21DDA (Proc. Pen. No. 20604/2010 R.G.N.R. Mod. 21DDA) n. 17375/11 R.G. GIP, (n. Richiesta di rinvio a giudizio) e n. 8338/2015 R.G. G.I.P. (n. Avviso Fissazione Udienza Preliminare).
24 See the dedicated website for the trials of 'Operation Aemilia'. Cf. www.processoaemilia.com/15-giugno-2016
25 Ibid. Prog. No. 59 RIT 1781/11.
26 Operazione Aemilia, Tribunale Ordinario di Bologna. Ordinanza di Applicazione di Misure Cautelari Coercitive, proc. no. 20604–10 RNR DDA – no. 17375–11 R GIP, p. 1240.
27 See in the news, November 3, 2017 – Cf. www.ilrestodelcarlino.it/reggio-emilia/cronaca/processo-aemilia-iaquinta-1.3542314
28 "Basta, io non sono un mafioso Volevo anche fuggire da Reggio" by Mike Scullin – Il Resto del Carlino – March 4, 2016 – Cf. www.ilrestodelcarlino.it/reggio-emilia/cronaca/ndrangheta-iaquinta-volevo-fuggire-1.1944417
29 Secondigliano is a suburb in the north of Naples where the camorra clan Grimaldi-Angrisano 'rule'.

30 Federazione Italiana Giuoco Calcio – FIGC – Press Release December 16, 2016 – Illecito Sportivo – Cf. www.figc.it/Assets/contentresources_2/ContenutoGenerico/44.$plit/C_2_ContenutoGenerico_2535496_Strillo AreaStampa_upfDownload.pdf
31 Interview in May 2017 in the DDA in Naples.
32 Operazione Rinnovamento ("Renewal") – no. 3748/13 RG GIP-Tribunale di Milano.
33 The *Arma dei Carabinieri* is one of the Italian police forces, under the Ministry of Defence.
34 Tribunale di Milano, Ufficio del Giudice per le Indagini Preliminari, Ordinanza di Custodia Cautelare, Proc. Pen. No. 12053/11 RGNR – No. 2877/11 RGGIP.
35 Operazione Rinnovamento ("Renewal") – no. 3748/13 RG GIP-Tribunale di Milano.
36 The daughter of former Prime Minister Silvio Berlusconi and chairwoman of Fininvest Holding and of the Arnoldo Mondadori Editore publishing group.
37 Interview to "Il Fatto Quotidiano" – February 7, 2017 – Cf. www.ilfattoquotidiano.it/2017/02/07/ndragheta-e-ultras-juventus-di-lello-societa-e-in-una-zona-grigia-valutiamo-se-ascoltare-i-dirigenti/3374198/
38 Operazione Alto Piemonte – Procura di Torino, Proc. Pen. No. 10270/09 RGNR DDA
39 Ibid.
40 The investigation is ongoing at the time of writing this book, and the Mafia & Sport committee of the Antimafia Commission were carrying out its auditions across various soccer clubs in the country.
41 Operazione Alto Piemonte – Procura di Torino, Proc. Pen. No. 10270/09 RGNR DDA.
42 'Juventus, caso biglietti-ultrà: la Corte d'Appello della Figc deciderà su Andrea Agnelli entro il 18 Dicembre'; cf. http://news.superscommesse.it/calcio/2017/12/juventus-caso-biglietti-ultra-la-corte-dappello-della-figc-decidera-su-andrea-agnelli-entro-il-18-dicembre-337735/
43 'Bagheria, scontro sullo stadio intestato al fratello del boss'; cf. http://palermo.repubblica.it/dettaglio/bagheria-scontro-sullo-stadio-intestato-al-fratello-del-boss/1570473
44 'Fabrizio Miccoli condannato per estorsione: tre anni e mezzo all'ex capitano del Palermo'; cf. www.lastampa.it/2017/10/20/sport/calcio/fabrizio-miccoli-condannato-per-estorsione-tre-anni-e-mezzo-allex-capitano-del-palermo-27edhwAqSJNeAFEL6BAOiL/pagina.html
45 'Indagato il presidente del Palermo Zamparini'; cf. www.lastampa.it/2017/07/29/sport/calcio/indagato-il-presidente-del-palermo-zamparini-FIoeW1SaxekhFzVpxqiCtJ/pagina.html

46 Tribunale penale di Catania, Sez I in composizione collegiale, No. 4305/14, RGNR no.11536/07.
47 Ibid., p. 13.
48 Operazione "I Treni del Gol", Procura di Catania, Proc. Pen. No. 5559/2015.
49 Ibid. Prog. No. 528 of 4.5.2015.
50 Federazione Italiana Giuoco Calcio – Tribunale Federale Nazionale – Sezione Disciplinare – Comunicato Ufficiale N. 15/Tfn, 20.08.2015, p. 8.
51 Authors' personal correspondence with prosecutor Alessandro Sorrentino in April 2017 – material not for public dissemination.
52 Sentence against Agliozzo Vito +12 –Tribunale Penale di Catania, Proc. Pen. No. 11536/07, Sentence No. 4305/14, deposited for archives 03.09.2015.
53 'Giorgio Chinaglia, Italian Star and the Cosmos' Leader, Dies at 65'; cf. www.nytimes.com/2012/04/03/sports/soccer/giorgio-chinaglia-italian-star-and-the-cosmos-leader-dies-at-65.html
54 Operazione Linea d'Ombra, Proc. Pen. No. 8318/2011 RGNR GIP, Tribunale di Salerno.
55 October 18, 2017, Alberto Gambino was acquitted by the Italian Corte di Cassazione (the Italian highest judicial authority); Cf. www.ansa.it/campania/notizie/2017/10/12/gambino-assoltocomplotto-contro-di-me_7900c19a-5893-4eb2-8ad0-b7bfedf4fc54.html
56 Legione Carabinieri 'Piemonte e Valle D'Aosta', Comando Provinciale di Torino, Reparto Operativo Nucleo Investigativo, 11 dicembre 2011, Proc. Pen. No. 6191/2007 RGNR DDA della Procura della Repubblica di Torino.
57 Operazione All Clean, April 21, 2011, Guardia di Finanza e Arma dei Carabinieri – Decreto di sequestro n. 91/2011 R.G.M.P. della Sezione Misure di Prevenzione del Tribunale di Reggio Calabria.
58 Operazione All Inside, Proc. Pen. No. 4302/06 RGNR DDA Reggio Calabria.
59 Tribunale Ordinario di Reggio Calabria, Sezione dei giudici per le indagini preliminari, Ordinanza di Convalida e Decreto di Sequestro Preventivo nei confronti di Arena Domenico +42, GIP Dott. Roberto Carrelli Palumbi, Proc. Pen. No. 4302/06 DDA Reggio Calabria ("All Inside"), September 29, 2011.
60 Operazione All Inside, Proc. Pen. No. 4302/06 RGNR DDA Reggio Calabria, Fermo di Indiziati di Delitto e Sequestro Preventivo in via d'urgenza, Trascrizione del colloquio del 25.01.2007 (RIT 2431/06 DDA) (vds. all. nr. 309 Vol. 2) – p. 316.

References

Allum, F., 2013. Godfathers, Dark Glasses, and Pasta: Discussing British Perceptions of Italian Mafias. *Sicurezza e scienze sociali*, 1(3), pp. 51–68.

Cantona, R. and Di Feo, G., 2012. *Soccer clan: Perché il calcio è diventato lo sport più amato dalle mafie*. Milano: BUR Biblioteca University Rizzoli.

Dickie, J., 2013. *Mafia Republic: Italy's Criminal Curse: Cosa Nostra, 'Ndrangheta and Camorra from 1946 to the Present*. London: Sceptre.

Di Ronco, A. and Lavorgna, A., 2015. Fair Play? Not So Much: Corruption in the Italian Soccer. *Trends in Organized Crime*, 18(3), pp. 176–195.

DNA, 2016. Relazione annuale sulle attività svolte dal Procuratore nazionale e dalla Direzione nazionale antimafia e antiterrorismo nonché sulle dinamiche e strategie della criminalità organizzata di tipo mafioso nel periodo 1° luglio 2014–30 giugno 2015. Roma: Direzione Nazionale Antimafia e Antiterrorismo.

Paoli, L., 2007. Mafia and Organised Crime in Italy: The Unacknowledged Successes of Law Enforcement. *West European Politics*, 30(4), pp. 854–880.

Paoli, L., 2003. *Mafia Brotherhoods: Organized Crime, Italian Style*. New York: Oxford University Press.

Prattico, N., 2014. La mafia al nord. Dal negazionismo alla presa di coscienza dell'esistenza del fenomenonelle forme della colonizzazione e delocalizzazione. *Questione Giustizia*, pp. 207–221.

Romani, P., 2012. Coppola e Pallone: calcio e criminalità. In: Ciconte, E., Forgione, F. and Sales, I. (eds.). *Atlante delle Mafie. Volume 1*. Soveria Mannelli: Rubbettino.

Sergi, A., 2017. *From Mafia to Organised Crime: A Comparative Analysis of Policing Models*. London; New York: Palgrave Macmillan.

Sergi, A. and Lavorgna, A., 2016. *'Ndrangheta: The Glocal Dimensions of the Most Powerful Italian Mafia*. London; New York: Palgrave Macmillan.

Transcrime, 2015. From Illegal Markets to Legitimate Businesses: The Portfolio of Organised Crime in Europe. In: Commission, E (ed.). *Organised Crime Portfolio*. Available: www.transcrime.it/wp-content/uploads/2015/03/OCP_Executive-Summary.pdf

Varese, F., 2011. *Mafias on the Move: How Organized Crime Conquers New Territories*. Princeton, NJ; Oxford: Princeton University Press.

Varese, F., 2005. *How Mafias Migrate: The Case of the 'Ndrangheta in Northern Italy*. Oxford: University of Oxford.

Chapter 5

'Ndrangheta and 'Dirty Soccer'

The interest of mafias in soccer at the local level is a manifestation of their power, as much as any other interest that clans nurture at the local level. As said earlier in this book, it is fundamental to understand the special relationship, the essential bond which mafia groups need to develop and maintain with their territory of origin. The control of territory is the crucial element of preserving consent because preserving consent means holding on to the governance over the territory. Governance over the territory requires acumen to seize opportunities for profit as well as the ability to maintain these opportunities' profitability through a tight network of contacts which are established and reinforced through the individual reputation of affiliates, and the collective reputation of the clan. The power of mafia groups is a power from below, which means that – and this is valid even when it comes to soccer – the *local* highly influences the *national*. Depending on the conditions found at the local level and the typologies of influence that mafia clans wish (often with great success) to exercise on soccer clubs or players or matches, there might be repercussions beyond the local. At the local level, mafia infiltration is linked to business opportunities as much as it is at the national level, even above being a matter of control of the territory.

As noticed in the 2016 Antimafia Commission's report on mafia infiltration in licit and illicit games (Vaccari, 2016, p. 43):

> The interests of mafia organisations in the world of soccer is not limited only to match-fixing and illegal betting, but it represents a useful

springboard to acquire electoral, economic and financial consensus. In particular soccer in the lower leagues attracts the clans, as it allows them to reinforce the ties with the territory and, in particular, with local entrepreneurs. The clans can, in some cases, impose rackets on local entrepreneurs through sponsorship of local teams or through other ways of involuntary financial support.

The links with the territory through different types of involvement with local soccer teams and local entrepreneurs, too, is a classical mafia mechanism, typical indeed of all mafias, provided we take a definition of mafia from a socio-behavioural perspective.[1] The acquisition of influence in local teams allows entrance into the market for activities such as match-fixing and illegal betting and the establishment of relationships with the social networks populating the soccer field. This is even more relevant at the local level and even more visible in smaller towns or villages, where relationships are tighter and roles and interests often overlap.

So far, the analysis has shown that, when it comes to soccer, there is no unique reason for which mafias choose to be involved. At all levels, micro, macro and meso, mafia clans invest according to strategic needs for their social status as well as business opportunities. The corruption-led fields of power that derive and benefit from mafia involvement are based on the strength of networks and the knowledge of the field rather than on strategic planning of infiltrating soccer specifically. Soccer, like many other business activities, is an opportunity to engage with lucrative and diverse activities linked with the possibility to reinforce the bonds in a given territory. However, the way each mafia (clan or organisation) acts within its territory surely will influence the interactions and the results of these interactions within the world of soccer.

The reputation of mafia clans and their reach at the local level does indeed influence the success of their soccer operations both locally and nationally, as 'Operation Dirty Soccer', a major Italian 'ndrangheta-linked match-fixing investigation, demonstrates. This chapter will examine Operation Dirty Soccer by presenting for the first time a qualitative analysis of its judicial documents, which include wiretaps and presentation of the evidence collected by antimafia prosecutors. The chapter will provide a historical framework of the investigation, its follow-up trials and preliminary results, but it will mainly look at what can be learned, challenged and confirmed through this operation.

It first must be said that Operation Dirty Soccer is by far not the most representative operation among those that exemplify the interests of mafia method and mafia interests in soccer. It is, however, an investigation that lets us see all the three levels, the micro, meso and macro levels, overlapping. We can, in fact, see in Operation Dirty Soccer how the *local* reputation of the 'ndrangheta represents the foundation for establishing match-fixing networks and corrupt soccer nationally and internationally.

With growing attention on the way the 'ndrangheta clans are socially embedded in the reality of the Calabria region as well as in wider Italy and abroad, it is crucial to look at the way the clans nourish social consensus as well as play their roles in the life of their communities via soccer and corruption-related practices. Finally, this chapter will demonstrate the importance of considering corruption as *habitus* in the mafia field; the more mafia clans are embedded in their communities, the more fluid corruption becomes.

Case study: 'Operation Dirty Soccer'

Background

As mentioned earlier, the operation named 'Dirty Soccer'[2] is an investigation conducted by the District Antimafia Prosecutors (DDA) in Catanzaro, Calabria, and executed by the police in Catanzaro and Rome. The investigation first started in 2009 and continued until 50 preliminary arrests were carried out on May 19, 2015. Under investigation were 84 people, and under trial, in November 2016, there were eventually 62, even though the investigation and prosecution had been split across different antimafia district offices in various Italian regions. This investigation converges many aspects of what has been discussed so far: the mix between corruption systems and mafia power on one side and the importance of the local environment for the exercise of mafia power on the other. Essentially, Dirty Soccer shows how the world of soccer in Italy has been consolidating a worrying orientation towards profit-making through legal and illegal channels. In this orientation, mafia connections, mafia cash and mafia reputation have been keys to securing the success of corruption schemes. In an attempt to summarise the operation, we can refer to the words of the Direzione Nazionale Antimafia in 2016 (DNA, 2016, p. 614):

> The investigations [. . .] were based on interceptions which led to the identification of criminal activities of two organised crime groups, separated from one another but sharing a subjective link. The two groups were dedicated to sport fraud and match-fixing in the amateur league [Serie D] as well as in professional soccer [Lega Pro]. The investigations have revealed a criminal underworld well established in the world of soccer, with 'professionals' in the field at the top. They exploited their functions within soccer clubs to fix matches during championships in order to alter results and obtain profits from their own betting on the events.

Antimafia prosecutor and chief investigator in Dirty Soccer in Catanzaro, Elio Romano,[3] specifies, however, that in 2017 Dirty Soccer was

> divided into 7 or 8 different antimafia prosecution directorates across Italy, with the majority of the investigation now moved to Rimini and Naples. [. . .] The most problematic feature of Dirty Soccer was the amount of money, like €100,000 each time, each bet, paid by Serbians or Croats, to bet on Italian soccer.

As the whole of the investigation started within another antimafia operation on the Iannazzo clan, Romano notes how

> At the beginning, the whole operation seemed to be mafia-related; then we found out about the second branch and things got more complicated and more diffused at national level. Even though the direct mafia connotation became less prominent, the mafia method was used throughout.

It is important to distinguish between the two groups the investigation focused on: not only were they two distinct systems, but they had different profiles in terms of 'membership', reach and *modus operandi*, including the use of the mafia method. Crucially, only the first group had a recognisable 'ndrangheta component, while the other could be generally understood as a system of corruption-led power, at times exploiting the mafia reputation. They both, however, presented certain characteristics. In fact, both groups pivoted around figures of *brokers*, managers and others who exploited their roles and functions in the world of soccer; they used their roles and functions and their networks to alter the scores and ensure illicit profits to coaches and/or players of other teams also willing to falsify their games.

The first group, which we can identify as the one with the mafia component, is best described as a triumvirate where three individuals shared the organisation of various activities to corrupt the championship of the Lega Nazionale Dilettanti, LND, Serie D – the amateur league. These were the president of the Neapolis (team in the metropolitan area of Naples), Mario Moxedano; director of the Neapolis, Antonio Ciccarrone; and Pietro Iannazzo, boss of the 'ndrangheta clan Iannazzo in Lamezia Terme, Calabria, already in prison for mafia offences at the time of the arrests for Dirty Soccer. He officially acted as a consultant for the Neapolis. The main aim of this first group was to ensure that the Neapolis won the Serie D championship. They also organised different types of fraud in tournaments of the same league, but where the Neapolis did not play, in order to boost profits, increase their visibility in the underworld and discourage competitors.

The second group, which we also can identify as the one with the transnational component, worked within the Lega Pro, the third league of professional soccer. Its 'master of ceremonies' is Fabio Di Lauro, a former Calabrian soccer player who acted as a 'dealmaker' within a network that comprised both national and transnational fraudsters. He claimed to have mafia links in Calabria, which, however, are not proven to be real. His main contacts at the national levels were the director of the team of l'Aquila, Ercole Di Nicola, and Daniele Ciardi of the team Santarcangelo. While their aim was to control the Lega Pro (third division) tournaments for the benefit of their own teams, they also 'sold' their services of match-fixing to other teams, including teams in the Lega Serie B (second division), when possible, and also in different parts of Italy. Fabio Di Lauro appears to have been the only broker in Italy for betters based in Serbia, Slovenia, Albania and Turkey. These betters were investors who demanded the fixing of the match they have bet on, often also online. One of them, as we will see, was believed to be close to 'ndrangheta clans in Calabria as well. Their interactions were not always 'pacific', as the investigation uncovered incidents of physical violence and altercations to settle debts across the country when some of the foreign investors/betters are involved.

The investigations into the first group led to the second group. In particular, the investigation started from an antimafia investigation, 'Operation Andromeda', against the Iannazzo clan, which led to the imprisonment of Pietro Iannazzo, among others.[4] While intercepting the communications of Pietro Iannazzo, the first group's network and activities emerged. Through the interceptions of Ciccarone, the authorities uncovered the involvement of Ercole Di Nicola and then Fabio Di Lauro. This was an important element not only to unite the two groups under the same investigation but also to explain why, afterwards, the cases were separated in preparation for different trials in different areas of Italy. The existence of interconnected styles and systems of corruption-led practices that exist and proliferate can clearly be seen in this investigation. In what the authorities have called the 'soccer underworld', eventually everyone meets.

The soccer underworld: crimes and charges

The intricate networks uncovered in this investigation point to several illicit actions that are both the proof of the stability of both groups and the result of this stability. The charges sustained by the Italian prosecutors stem both from evidence of crimes related to soccer and crimes unrelated to it. In the bulk of the investigation, we find activities to corrupt the fairness and the honesty of the games by fixing the matches and altering the scores. In the remaining part of the investigation we find activities such as extortion, corruption, kidnapping for ransom and possession of illegal weapons.

As explained and summarised by the press release[5] issued by the police headquarters in Catanzaro, Calabria, in 2015 upon executing the arrests:

> It has been ascertained that the two groups were managed with the same 'modus operandi'. In particular, the most important members of both groups – all holding high positions and important organisational roles within their groups – did use their own contacts and networks to approach players who might be available to agree to the fixing or the alteration of a match in exchange for money or promises of more remunerative roles in other teams.

The match-fixing system in place was participated in by managers, coaches and football players of different teams from local and national leagues, and the systems thrived on the exploitation of particular difficulties of the soccer industry as well as technicalities of the betting game. In particular, as it said in the official press release:[6]

> We also ascertained a particular capacity of these two networks of defendants in taking advantage, for their own profit, of economic difficulties suffered by some teams, which, because of these difficulties, appeared more available to accept bribes and gains coming from the fixing of matches as disposed by the criminal networks. Debts, in fact, compromise a team's position in the league, thus making the same team more permeable to illicit offers of match alterations. In particular, the more peculiar the results of the altered match (for example with a specific number of goals from both teams) the more the team increased their gain, due to the betting being connected on the numbers of goals, for example.

The evidence against the first criminal network supported filing charges of sport fraud in 11 matches in the amateur league (LND), while the evidence against the second network supported charges for 14 matches in the Lega Pro (third division). Local teams from the southern regions of Calabria, Campania, and Puglia were mostly involved in playing the matches fixed by the first group, while the reach of the second group in the professional league included teams in the north and centre of Italy, in regions like Liguria, Toscana, Veneto, Lombardia, Lazio and Abruzzo. Description and analysis of some of the intercepted conversations in both groups will provide further insight into how the evidence of the match-fixing was gathered and constructed against both groups, both within and outside areas of mafia influence.

First group: Brindisi-San Severo

Let's initially see the first group in action, for the match Brindisi-San Severo, Serie D (amateur league), played on November 30, 2014, with a final result (as fixed) of 2–1. The fixing apparently happened through a preliminary arrangement between Antonio Ciccarone and William Carotenuto, goalkeeper of San Severo, where the latter agreed to fake his performance during the match. Once this agreement was in place, Ciccarone discussed further details with the technical consultant, Savino Daleno; the manager, Vito Marisco; and the president and vice-president of Brindisi, Antonio and Giorgio Flora, who would be paying Carotenuto for his 'support'. On the brokers' side, Vinicio Ciccarone, brother of Antonio, would represent the network and collect the money at the end of the match. They would also bet on the matches themselves and invite others to do it, so as to increase profits for themselves and their 'friends'. Through the interceptions we can follow the unfolding of this part of the story. In particular, the following excerpts build up to reveal the role of Antonio Ciccarone as broker and the existing relationships and interests at play, as delineated by the prosecutors.

Excerpt no. 1[7]

William CAROTENUTO: Hey big leader!
Antonio CICCARONE: It's almost Christmas!
William CAROTENUTO: Eh . . . I am only here until Monday, what can we do?

Antonio CICCARONE: We are in trouble . . . really in trouble . . . in trouble as it's Christmas and we don't have any money! We need to do something . . .

William CAROTENUTO: Of course, shall we see what we can do?

Excerpt no. 2[8]

Antonio CICCARONE: Oh . . . what did I want to say?? I have seen the boy, the one you asked me about . . . .

Savino DALENO: Yes . . .

Antonio CICCARONE: Eeeh . . . tell me something, we need to meet up as he comes too and I cannot do next week . . . so we need to meet up like tomorrow . . . I can also talk a bit, then you can talk to him, I'll introduce you . . . you talk to him and you'll see . . . It's a good player eh . . . a good player . . . I've been told he is as well . . . so . . . (. . .)

Savino DALENO: OK, so when can we meet?

Antonio CICCARONE: Tomorrow we can meet . . . whenever you say it, I'll swing by . . .

Excerpt no. 3[9]

Savino DALENO: Vito

Vito MORISCO: Oh hi, so?

Savino DALENO: All good, all good! I'm on my way . . . I'm going to meet a friend . . .

Vito MORISCO: Ah, I see, I see!

Savino DALENO: They told me there is this one [he calls him 'Under', in code] . . . he's good . . . but there's a price to pay . . . I said OK, I'm coming, we'll see . . .

Vito MORISCO: I see

Savino DALENO: See? And I am going . . .

Vito MORISCO: OK then, talk later.

Excerpt no. 4[10]

Savino DALENO: Hello?

William CAROTENUTO: Savino, good morning, it's William Carotenuto.

Savino DALENO: Ciao William . . .
William CAROTENUTO: How are you?
Savino DALENO: All good, all good
William CAROTENUTO: Everything OK?
Savino DALENO: Yes . . .
William CAROTENUTO: OK, good, yes, but the little contract? What about the little contract? [He calls their money agreement 'contrattino' – little contract.]
Savino DALENO: Yes, we'll do it by the end of today . . . OK? I have spoken to Antonio [Ciccarone]
William CAROTENUTO: How, by the end of today?
Savino DALENO: OK . . .?
William CAROTENUTO: Eh, OK I see, but how does it work?
Savino DALENO: I will meet Antonio . . . I will meet Antonio and then he will meet you so you can . . . sign.

Second group: Juve Stabia-Lupa Roma

The second group mainly organised match-fixing in the Lega Pro (third division), and at times also in the second division, Serie B (for example Livorno-Brescia, played on January 24, 2015, with a final score, as fixed, 4–2; see later in this chapter). The *modus operandi* of the second group was stable throughout. The network counted on the knowledge and insider trading of information from Ercole Di Nicola, manager of L'Aquila team, very well connected in the world of soccer. Through his tight network of relationships and information, he was able to influence matches by approaching players directly, like the first group did.

In addition to national contacts, and different from the first group, they also befriended foreign investors that funded their activities in exchange for safe bets. For example, in the event of the match Juve Stabia-Lupa Roma on November 1, 2014, Ercole Di Nicola was willing to 'sell' the fixed score (1–0, final result as agreed) of the match to his foreign investors in exchange for an easy, but substantial, sum of money (€8,000). The name of Di Nicola seemed to be a constant in soccer scandals; as mentioned in chapter 1 of this book, he was linked to

Nobile Capuani in 2017 and the alleged match-fixing occurring in Spain involving the Eldense Soccer Club (Segunda B division). In this event of Dirty Soccer, even though the connection between Di Nicola and the foreign investors (in particular Michele Jovicic) was autonomous, the role of Fabio Di Lauro remained central to the 'reputation' and the functioning of the criminal group, as the investors counted on him to guarantee that their bet was safe. Also, Di Lauro double-checked on Di Nicola (at times using the mafia method of intimidation, as we will see in the next section of this chapter) that the information purchased is solid. The excerpts from the interceptions below show how the agreement was made very quickly (within a couple of days prior to the match and finalised on the day of the match) and how the question of trust between Di Lauro and Di Nicola was central and prodromal to these types of agreements.

Excerpt no. 5[11]

Ercole DI NICOLA: Morning
Michele JOVICIC: Good morning my friend . . . so can you tell me if we play 'one'[12] for that Juve [Stabia] 'boy'?
Ercole DI NICOLA: Yes . . .
Michele JOVICIC: OK then, I will call you back in about two hours, OK?
Ercole DI NICOLA: Do you have anything for me?
Michele JOVICIC: Not yet, no . . . but in two hours I might . . .

Excerpt no. 6[13]

Ercole DI NICOLA: Yes
Michele JOVICIC: Ercò . . . we have an agreement for 8 thousand OK? On 'one'.
Ercole DI NICOLA: All right . . .
Michele JOVICIC: 'One' we have to play, 'one'. . .
Ercole DI NICOLA: Anything else?
Michele JOVICIC: Nothing . . .
   (. . .)
Ercole DI NICOLA: Ah . . .

Michele JOVICIC: OK, let's say that if you lose you owe us 8 thousand . . . but I bet 8 that we win. We meet tonight and I'll give it to you . . . ok?

Excerpt no. 7[14]

Michele JOVICIC: Ercò . . .
Ercole DI NICOLA: Speaking . . .
Michele JOVICIC: So, we have an agreement that the Juve [Stabia] wins, right?
Ercole DI NICOLA: Yes, why?
Michele JOVICIC: He has already bet 'one'. . . so it's to double check that we put 'one'. . . or 'two'?[15] . . . we put 'one' OK?
Ercole DI NICOLA: Yes, yes
Michele JOVICIC: OK, so we speak tonight . . .

Excerpt no. 8[16]

Daniele CIARDI: Mate!
Fabio DI LAURO: Danié
Daniele CIARDI: Hey
Fabio DI LAURO: I think that Ercole . . . if the match he told them about doesn't go through . . . I think they'll kill him . . .
Daniele CIARDI: Why? Which match?
Fabio DI LAURO: Eh . . . he said . . . he made them bet on the Juve Stabia . . .
Daniele CIARDI: OK . . . then . . . when are they playing?
Fabio DI LAURO: At 5. . . I have been with them until now [. . .] They have put 30/40 thousand Euros on the Juve Stabia . . . jeez . . . crazy Danié . . . crazy . . . because he told them . . . and they asked me . . . I called Ercole . . . and I said . . .
Daniele CIARDI: Mmm . . .
Fabio DI LAURO: I said, "Ercole" I said . . . "but what you told them, is that right? I mean, they are not risking it, right?". . . "Fabio", he says, "what are you saying?". . . "Ercole, what you told them" . . . "OK, whatever, I am hanging up" and he hung up! And I think that OK . . . boh . . .
Daniele CIARDI: What can I tell you . . . .

The role of 'ndrangheta *habitus* in soccer corruption

The first group counted on the outspoken support of the 'ndrangheta clan to which Pietro Iannazzo belongs. The first group, therefore, added a mafia connotation to their whole soccer business. However, also in the second group, Fabio Di Lauro, of Calabrian origins, claimed a connection to 'ndrangheta clans, which however, cannot be proved further. These two manifestations of mafia power can be explained within the framework that sees mafia as *habitus* rather than solely a criminal organisation or a set of criminal activities. In both examples from Dirty Soccer, mafia power is manifested by social practices based primarily on the importance and influence of the brand name (of the 'ndrangheta) and on the strength of the *reputation* of the Calabrian clans. Within the mafia/'ndrangheta power field, symbolic and social capital is more important than merely economic capital. Reputation, added to the access to territory and people, through those instrumental friendships described in literature (Blok, 1988), is the added value to the systems of corruption that make 'Dirty Soccer':

> As noted by the antimafia prosecutors,[17] about what concerned the first criminal group:
>
>> From the interception of the phone line used by Pietro Iannazzo (no. 859/13) it emerged how he used his criminal calibre as a key member of the 'ndrangheta clan by employing his surname and his knowledge of different individuals in Calabrian soccer clubs. This way, he had managed to establish a network of 'characters' all connected to each other, which worked through a system of 'mutual assistance'. The final aim was influencing some of the scores of soccer matches within the LND, Serie D, for which it was also possible to place regular bets through authorised means.

Pietro Iannazzo's calibre and personal connections are considered the essence of the mafia *habitus* in this case. It is fundamental to point out that the reason why Iannazzo's presence and support was successful was essentially due to the pre-existing prestige of the Iannazzo clan, based in Lamezia Terme and considered by the prosecutors in separate proceedings.[18] The clan has been fully operative since 2003 in the central part of Calabria and has a typical hierarchical structure: "The clan, through the strategic figure of Pietro Iannazzo, has the capability of penetrating into unsuspected ganglions of civil society, aiming at gaining illicit profits to benefit the collective criminal plan."[19]

In 'Dirty Soccer', we can see how the reputation of the clan, on the one hand, calls for the usual behaviour of *deference* from outsiders and, on the other hand, is deeply rooted in the importance of the name as a guarantee of power. Reputation is tightly linked to the concept of *honour* – both are two of the most important values of any mafia *doxa*. This, for the 'ndrangheta – based on kinship and blood – is even more relevant. With reputation comes the access to a network that can guarantee 'entry' in the territory. This is quite visible in a conversation between Pietro Iannazzo and Antonio Ciccarone, on the occasion of a meeting to discuss their partnership.

Excerpt no. 9[20]

Pietro IANNAZZO: Boss . . .
Antonio CICCARONE: Pietro . . .
Pietro IANNAZZO: Tell me.
Antonio CICCARONE: So, when we speak about those aspects and we go into details of the situations, we can say that it's beyond Calabria . . . where we have certain situations like an example, like for Hinterreggio or Roccella . . . we have the fields available, right?
Pietro IANNAZZO: Yes
Antonio CICCARONE: You know, for the trainings and all, you tell him [to Mario Moxedano] what the situation is, we can . . . we can do it . . . (. . .)
Pietro IANNAZZO: Don't worry . . . I will . . .
Antonio CICCARONE: Yeah, good . . . no, the important thing is that when we get to details you need to let him see that "President, I feel like . . . from now it's like I am part of your family"
Pietro IANNAZZO: Yeah, it's like that, because if it's not . . .

Antonio CICCARONE: Good, if it's not, you say "President, if I'm not part of your family, then I am not the one you thought I was?"

Pietro IANNAZZO: No . . .

Antonio CICCARONE: Do you get it?

Pietro IANNAZZO: Yeah, it's not my style, right?

Antonio CICCARONE: Good then

Pietro IANNAZZO: I am investing my name here!

Antonio CICCARONE: And you need to say that "independently from everything else we need to plan the first steps", you need to say! "It's December, and in December half of the championship is gone, you can watch our work in the making and then you'll see." Our! Say yours, mine . . . you and I! "You can evaluate that . . ." Do you see what I am saying?

Pietro IANNAZZO: Yeah, sure.

Another aspect of mafia power that can be identified in Dirty Soccer, and precisely in the activities of the second group, is specifically linked to the current popularity and peak of reputation of the 'ndrangheta. It has been argued elsewhere (Sergi, 2016; Sergi and Lavorgna, 2016) that organised crime groups of Calabrian origins are today undergoing a process of *'ndranghetisation*, locally, nationally and internationally. By 'ndranghetisation, we refer to a process for which criminals who have a connection with Calabria – whichever part of Calabria – might claim an affiliation to the 'ndrangheta to boost their credibility and benefit of the strong (criminal) reputation of the Calabrian mafia. This process can be initiated, or confirmed and facilitated, by media or policy makers who fail to understand the different nuances of the Calabrian clans and tend to aggregate all organised criminals with a connection to Calabria to the 'ndrangheta. In any case, the 'ndranghetisation process transfers the reputation of the 'ndrangheta clans as reliable, wealthy and powerful criminal organisations to various and different criminal networks to boost their own reach in the territory and in criminal markets (usually outside Calabria). This process confirms that the 'ndrangheta, as previously said in this chapter, is not just intended as the unitary criminal organisation from the province of Reggio

Calabria, but it is indeed intended as a *habitus*, a tacit way of *doing* and *being* mafioso in Calabria. This is perfectly visible in the attitude of Fabio Di Lauro, central figure of the second group in Dirty Soccer. In the events leading to the match-fixing of Juve Stabia-Lupa Roma seen earlier, the interceptions reveal how Di Lauro's centrality in the network, especially with the foreign investors/partners, also is re-affirmed, thanks to his proclaimed proximity to 'ndrangheta clans in Calabria, due essentially to his Calabrian origin. The nature of these links cannot however be confirmed. The text message here was sent by Fabio Di Lauro to Ercole Di Nicola:[21] it is revealing of the relationship between the two, of Di Lauro's alleged links with the 'ndrangheta, as well as the foreigners' links with the 'ndrangheta as a vehicle to claim respect and honour.

> They are my friends, don't think they act without me. There is a friendship of people from Calabria, close to me and close to them, show some respect . . . so don't try alone, I was with them just yesterday.

Dirty Soccer, corruption 'ndrangheta style

One of the characteristics of Dirty Soccer, apart from the 'impressive' results achieved by the two networks, relates to the fact that corruption in most of the narrated events is carried out in different styles, among which are the trafficking of favours, offers of mutual benefits and assistance, practices of illegal brokerage, briberies, illegal pacts, and mafia-inspired violence or threats of violence to ensure compliance.

We certainly agree with the words of antimafia prosecutor Michele Prestipino in Rome,[22] according to whom "We need to differentiate between corruptive systems and mafia systems, as they are different in purpose and style" – the former is based on the power of mutual illicit exchanges and the second is based on the power of intimidation and reputation. Obviously, these styles at times might converge and overlap. In Dirty Soccer, styles of corruption might include the employment of the 'mafia method' even beyond the 'official' involvement of mafia groups.

There are a number of very long extracts from the interceptions that would be very helpful to illustrate the different styles in which corruption of various individuals occurred to fix the scores for the matches and/or secure the bets. To keep the focus on the mafia aspect, we can focus on the events and the characters surrounding the (failed) match-fixing for Hinterreggio-Neapolis of 07.09.2014, organised by the first criminal group – the 'ndrangheta-led group. In this case, Pietro Iannazzo handled the various stages of the group's activities by approaching different individuals who might be helpful in securing the match. Among these are Mauro Ruga, FIFA agent and lawyer, and Pasquale Lo Giudice, manager of the Juve Stabia. Ruga and Lo Giudice were approached to provide contact with Fabio Caserta, shareholder of the Hinterreggio and former player of the Juve Stabia, in order to 'persuade' him, by offering adequate compensation to fix the match for the Neapolis to win. This is an event that shows how intermediation and brokerage worked for the first criminal network. The first important contact was between Iannazzo and Ruga, who know each other and are both from Calabria. Ruga was also implicated in a separate investigation for the proximity of his legal activity to the Ruga clan in the hinterland of Reggio Calabria.[23] Ruga agreed to facilitate a meeting between Iannazzo and Pasquale Lo Giudice in the days before the match. Before the meeting, Iannazzo discussed with his partner, Antonio Ciccarone, the necessity to pay 'the guy' adequately, where 'the guy' is a third person who would agree to the 'transfer' (meaning agreeing to support the fixed result). The cycle was closed when, after Iannazzo and Ciccarone discussed this, Ciccarone would agree with Moxedano about the 'funding', that is the amount of money to 'invest' in the corruptive pact arranged by Iannazzo. The following dialogue between Iannazzo and Ciccarone, after Iannazzo had spoken to Pasquale Lo Giudice, shows the different types of relationships and the style of the corruptive pact.

Excerpt no. 10[24]

Pietro IANNAZZO: . . . So . . . I have spoken with Pasquale . . .
Antonio CICCARONE: Yes
     (. . .)
Pietro IANNAZZO: He told me tomorrow . . .[. . .]

Antonio CICCARONE: Perfect
Pietro IANNAZZO: So, I'll be waiting for a call tonight, or tomorrow morning to agree whether you are coming for another meeting . . .
Antonio CICCARONE: Perfect
Pietro IANNAZZO: To agree on the transfer . . .
Antonio CICCARONE: That's OK anyway, so let's sum up, you went to speak with the mister [the manager – Lo Giudice]
Pietro IANNAZZO: Yes
Antonio CICCARONE: The mister guaranteed you someone . . .
Pietro IANNAZZO: Who will . . .
Antonio CICCARONE: In particular?
Pietro IANNAZZO: Yes, so . . . let's say I am aiming at 110% security, he gave me 99%, also because the guy we want, the guys actually . . .
Antonio CICCARONE: Yes
Pietro IANNAZZO: They are ready, they are 'under' [they have minor influence]
Antonio CICCARONE: Yes, yes
Pietro IANNAZZO: The 'over' have not signed yet, so I am not sure if they will by Sunday . . . the two we would want to transfer, you know.
Antonio CICCARONE: But one of the two is XXX's friend right?
Pietro IANNAZZO: Yes, it's him and that one is not the problem, he already gave him his word but he hasn't signed yet . . .
[. . .]
Pietro IANNAZZO: The other needs a bit of persuasion, which I am trying to do so he signs . . .
Antonio CICCARONE: Yes
Pietro IANNAZZO: So, you can be reassured that we will get to the transfer as I already laid all the ground work . . . the bases are there, but I want 110% and I will get it.
[. . .]
Pietro IANNAZZO: He is available, he will arrange the transfer, he knows that I will help him for the rest of the year if he is interested in some player too . . .
Antonio CICCARONE: No doubt
Pietro IANNAZZO: No doubt indeed

Antonio CICCARONE: And if the President [Moxedano] asks me how much we need for this transfer?

Pietro IANNAZZO: You and I will arrange that . . .

Antonio CICCARONE: Yes, but if he asks . . . just to get an idea . . .

Pietro IANNAZZO: Six-seven, maybe five-six [thousand Euro]

Antonio CICCARONE: OK so . . . I will say something higher . . .

Pietro IANNAZZO: Bravo

Antonio CICCARONE: So we can see . . . .

Pietro IANNAZZO: Yes perfect

Other conversations between the two are even more revealing of the fixing of the prices, the mutual assistance and the trafficking of favours.

Excerpt no. 11[25]

Pietro IANNAZZO: You know I am already arranging for other things too . . . but now I am all focused on this situation.

Antonio CICCARONE: This one is fundamental

Pietro IANNAZZO: Yeah, as if I were superficial . . .

Antonio CICCARONE: You know that if we start on the right foot we have done a splendid job with him [Moxedano].

Pietro IANNAZZO: Perfect.

Antonio CICCARONE: This is why I insist.

Pietro IANNAZZO: OK, OK.

Antonio CICCARONE: If he asks me whether we have talked about the transfer for the guys . . . I'll say "President, you need to give me a maximum, let's say of ten [thousand]". . . . Pietro is good, so he might be able to save some money anyway.

Pietro IANNAZZO: OK, OK great.

Antonio CICCARONE: OK then, I will say "give me a maximum of 10 and then if Pietro is good we will try and save money, and I am sure Pietro will want to show you he is good" . . . but it depends on how it evolves . . .

Pietro IANNAZZO: Va bene, OK, perfect!

[. . .]

Pietro IANNAZZO: So I just had lunch with Mauro Ruga . . .

Antonio CICCARONE: Yes

Pietro IANNAZZO: He called him [Pasquale Lo Giudice] and told him pretty much what I want with the transfer and if he could speak to his player; he said yes and as he knows I can help and it's something good for him [the player] too, he said to move quickly. So he's waiting for me tomorrow at 11 at the field.

[. . .]

Antonio CICCARONE: OK, you sound relaxed . . . do you think I should be coming too? You tell me . . .

Pietro IANNAZZO: Well, he talks to me fully, frankly, I am not sure . . . maybe not . . .

Antonio CICCARONE: So, OK, you know what, you go . . .

Pietro IANNAZZO: Yeah, I'll go and then we see . . .

Antonio CICCARONE: But you know . . . you need to tell him beyond what we'll do in this case to help, as I know they are struggling, so we help them this time, also later on – not just your friendships, but also mine will be helpful to them . . .

Pietro IANNAZZO: Sure, sure of course!

The 'player' Iannazzo and Ciccarone were discussing regarding an agreement with Lo Giudice was Fabio Caserta, a former Juve Stabia player who is also a shareholder of the Hinterreggio and therefore can help with the specific match. The following interceptions prior to the match show how Iannazzo and Ciccarone consider Caserta quite reliable and are happy with the agreement at the point that they start 'selling' the bet and betting themselves. When the match does not go as fixed and Hinterreggio eventually wins 2–0, Pietro Iannazzo's disappointment in a conversation with his friend Bobo, the organiser of the bets, reveals, in the view of the prosecutors, his *'ndranghetist habitus* by threatening repercussions bizarrely in the name of honour.

Excerpt no. 12[26]

Bobo (MAZZEI ANTONIO): 1–0?

Pietro IANNAZZO: 2–0

Bobo (MAZZEI ANTONIO): Two?
Pietro IANNAZZO: Clowns, they are clowns!
Bobo (MAZZEI ANTONIO): Shit . . .
Pietro IANNAZZO: You cannot find serious people, really . . . there are no serious people left!
Bobo (MAZZEI ANTONIO): Madness . . .
Pietro IANNAZZO: Bah . . . I don't know . . .
Bobo (MAZZEI ANTONIO): Did you call the guy [Fabio Caserta]. . . to tell him?
Pietro IANNAZZO: He was there!
Bobo (MAZZEI ANTONIO): Oh well!
Pietro IANNAZZO: We'll see now . . .
Bobo (MAZZEI ANTONIO): Compliment him!
Pietro IANNAZZO: I already did. I told him I will see him soon and all will be settled.
Bobo (MAZZEI ANTONIO): Eh?
Pietro IANNAZZO: Yes, soccer is a 'man of honour'!

According to the antimafia prosecutors, all the individuals identified in the first group allegedly committed the crimes attested to them in conspiracy as an organised crime group with the aggravating factor provided by article 7 of the law 203/91, which refers to the knowledge that their conspiracy was beneficial to a pre-existing mafia group, the clan Iannazzo. However, article 7 also provides for an aggravating factor to be contested when individuals use the mafia method to carry out a variety of crimes, independently from their actual affiliation to a mafia group, and provided that they realise the mafia intent: instilling fear, through the use of intimidation and threats based on the reputation and the reach of the criminal network (Sergi, 2017).

What Dirty Soccer has revealed in terms of mafia power in the world of soccer – independently from the individual positions and sentences at trial – goes beyond the involvement of an individual close to the clan and using his clan's reputation to forge connections useful for corruptive purposes. For the second criminal group investigated in Dirty Soccer, in fact, we have seen how Fabio Di Lauro claimed links with mafia groups in

Calabria to augment his credibility and instil reverential awe or fear. Di Lauro's friendships and reach were as central for the network as they were varied: for example, he could count on the support of Alberto Scarnà,[27] superintendent of the police in Ravenna, also Calabrian of origin, who not only participated in the betting but also covered up criminal activities he should instead have reported.

Last but not least, according to the prosecutors, a very interesting connection can be drawn between the element of transnationality of the second network and the existence of mafia interests, whether real or proclaimed/alleged. For example, the authorities knew that in the group of foreign investors from various Eastern European countries, the Slovenian, Uros Mirosavljevic, was the one to monitor for his importance and centrality in the network. Mirosavljevic, apart from holding a very clear role of leadership within his own network and showing a tendency to violence (he was also charged with possession of weapons), also seemed to be close to some Calabrian clans. Even though there were no further details on this in the investigation, the conditions of Mirosavljevic's proximity to a clan of the 'ndrangheta were known to the authorities and to Fabio Di Lauro who, as discussed before, reminded Ercole Di Nicola about his own connections to the Calabrian clans as well as theirs (the '*foreigners*'). The connections with the 'ndrangheta were indeed also the extra guarantee of seriousness and dangerousness of the second network in Dirty Soccer. These allegations of mafia connections also cost Mirosavljevic an aggravated charge within the previously mentioned article 7 law 203/91, because he allegedly acted by using techniques of intimidation on the basis of his vicinity to a 'ndrangheta clan.

Conclusion

In conclusion, and to re-iterate what has been said before, the mafia influence and the manifestations of mafia behaviours are by far not the main characteristic of Dirty Soccer, which has been nevertheless one of the largest investigations into the corruption of professional soccer in Italy. According to the files of the case,[28] the corruption mechanisms unveiled in Dirty Soccer are successful because:

> Every individual involved in the investigation, to different extents, abuses their function by turning this function into an instrument for particular personal ambitions and greedy economic interests. Every defendant exploits his role and builds networks based on corruption or potential corruption, where everyone can become both the promoter and the beneficiary of the system, in terms of economic gain or social prestige, within the different soccer communities of reference.

More importantly, note the extremely lucid and almost aggressive judgements of the prosecutors in the foreword of the case:

> Every time these individuals perfect one of their frauds, they insult the principles of probity, honesty, fairness and respect of the rules of the game as well as respect of the adversary they play against. By participating in the sport event this way, as well, they offend the good faith of the public that pays to attend the event as well as of those who bet legally. In their wrongdoings, these individuals become unfaithful, they betray their one function and the social reason of sport, in an absolute sense, by bending them to personal unjustifiable economic interests.

Certainly this type and these levels of corruption in football are a mirror of a much more widespread problem, which hits soccer but arguably has nothing to do with soccer. This is what Dirty Soccer essentially reveals, also from the foreword:

> In a country where public opinion is more and more aware and concerned about corruption in general, frauds in football realise a form of corruption among private actors, which even when it is punished, reveals, unfortunately, how much this world of soccer is rotten, with unscrupulous speculators who are willing to sell all they can and that really have nothing to share with sport.

Notwithstanding the corruption-led nature of these illicit networks, mafia influence and mafia interests – the mafia *habitus* – appear to be supplementary and complimentary to the corruption systems in the soccer field. As noted by antimafia prosecutor Elio Romano during our interview on Dirty Soccer: "different social groups use the mafia method, exhibit a mafia behaviour, for different aims, different even from those of mafias". Indeed, we can see in Dirty Soccer how both the involvement of members of mafia clans and the employment of the mafia *method* and reputation (in this case distinctively linked to the 'ndrangheta) are easily subsumed within the use of corruption as *doxa* in the soccer field; they change these mechanisms by adding the 'mafia-style' connotation. This connotation is essentially the mafia *habitus*: the offering of money and of suitable networks and personal connections; relying on reputation and on collective and individual intimidation derived from that reputation; and certainly exploiting their grip over certain territories to establish, maintain and foster successful criminal and non-criminal ventures. It must be remembered that the identification, or the manifestation, of the mafia *habitus* does not necessarily correspond to the existence of a mafia association. Violence, intimidation, threats, corruption and/or extortion can become mafia violence, mafia intimidation, mafia-style threat, mafia-supported corruption and/or mafia-led extortion as they manifest a more penetrating, energetic and efficient character. This character originates from the prospect that all these activities might contribute to, might lead to, or might originate from a criminal syndicate – the mafia clan – which is poly-crime and poly-location. Once the mafia method is used in support of other different types of criminal activities in a given territory or industry, the result is that mafia influence resonates more as the reputation of the clan grows. This ultimately feeds into the very core of mafia power: its origins in personal contacts, local influence and the generalised sense of impunity and grandeur.

Notes

1 C.f. Cantona, R. and Di Feo, G., 2012. *Footballclan: Perché il calcio è diventato lo sport più amato dalle mafie*. Milano: BUR Biblioteca University Rizzoli, and Romani, P., 2012. *Coppola e Pallone: calcio e criminalità*. In: Ciconte, E., Forgione, F. and Sales, I. (eds.). Atlante delle Mafie. Volume 1. Soveria Mannelli: Rubbettino.

2 Operazione Dirty Soccer, Procura della Repubblica presso il Tribunale di Catanzaro Direzione Distrettuale Antimafia (DDA) Proc. Pen. No. 1110/09 R.G.N.R.
3 Interview with Anna Sergi in April 2017 in Catanzaro.
4 Operazione Andromeda I & II – Ordinanza di Custodia Cautelare in Carcere – Proc. Pen. No. 1110/09 RGNR, no. 267/2010 RG. GIP – no. 167/14 RMC. Pietro Iannazzo has been convicted to 14 years and 8 months' imprisonment in February 2017 in the first degree trial.
5 Questura di Catanzaro, Comunicato Stampa, Operazione "Dirty Soccer", Catanzaro 19 maggio 2015, p. 3.
6 Ibid.
7 Allegato 214 dell'informativa di reato Prot. 200/2015/Mob/SCO_A/RM – Proc. Pen. No. 1110/09 R.G.N.R. MOD. 21, 03.11.2015 (27 days before the match).
8 Allegato 218 dell'informativa di reato Prot. 200/2015/Mob/SCO_A/RM – Proc. Pen. No. 1110/09 R.G.N.R. MOD. 21, 25.11.2015 (five days before the match).
9 Allegato 225 dell'informativa di reato Prot. 200/2015/Mob/SCO_A/RM – Proc. Pen. No. 1110/09 R.G.N.R. MOD. 21, 26.11.2014 (four days before the match).
10 Allegato 267 dell'informativa di reato Prot. 200/2015/Mob/SCO_A/RM – Proc. Pen. No. 1110/09 R.G.N.R. MOD. 21, 01.12.2014 (one day after the match).
11 Allegato 384 dell'informativa di reato Prot. 200/2015/Mob/SCO_A/RM – Proc. Pen. No. 1110/09 R.G.N.R. MOD. 21, 01.11.2014 (day of the match).
12 Playing 1 means that the bet is on the victory of the home team.
13 Allegato 385 dell'informativa di reato Prot. 200/2015/Mob/SCO_A/RM – Proc. Pen. No. 1110/09 R.G.N.R. MOD. 21, 01.11.2014 (day of the match).
14 Allegato 386 dell'informativa di reato Prot. 200/2015/Mob/SCO_A/RM – Proc. Pen. No. 1110/09 R.G.N.R. MOD. 21, 01.11.2014 (day of the match).
15 Playing 2 means that the bet is on the victory of the guest team.
16 Allegato 393 dell'informativa di reato Prot. 200/2015/Mob/SCO_A/RM – Proc. Pen. No. 1110/09 R.G.N.R. MOD. 21, 01.11.2014 (day of the match).
17 Proc. Pen. No. 1110/09 R.G.N.R. MOD. 21. Procura della Repubblica presso il Tribunale di Catanzaro, DDA. Fermo di indiziato di delitto, p. 30.
18 Operazione Andromeda I & II – Ordinanza di Custodia Cautelare in Carcere – Proc. Pen. No. 1110/09 RGNR, no. 267/2010 RG. GIP – no. 167/14 RMC.

19 Proc. Pen. No. 1110/09 R.G.N.R. MOD. 21. Procura della Repubblica presso il Tribunale di Catanzaro, DDA. Fermo di indiziato di delitto, p. 1260.
20 Allegato 2 dell'informativa di reato Prot. 200/2015/Mob/SCO_A/RM – Proc. Pen. No. 1110/09 R.G.N.R. MOD. 21.
21 Allegato 397 dell'informativa di reato Prot. 200/2015/Mob/SCO_A/RM – Proc. Pen. No. 1110/09 R.G.N.R. MOD. 21.
22 Interview with the one of the authors – Procura della Repubblica di Rome, April 2017.
23 Proc. Pen. No. 1110/09 R.G.N.R. MOD. 21. Procura della Repubblica presso il Tribunale di Catanzaro, DDA. Fermo di indiziato di delitto, p. 46.
24 Allegato 9 dell'informativa di reato Prot. 200/2015/Mob/SCO_A/RM – Proc. Pen. No. 1110/09 R.G.N.R. MOD. 21., 02.09.2014, 5 days before the match.
25 Allegato 10;12;15 dell'informativa di reato Prot. 200/2015/Mob/SCO_A/RM – Proc. Pen. No. 1110/09 R.G.N.R. MOD. 21.
26 Allegato 44 dell'informativa di reato Prot. 200/2015/Mob/SCO_A/RM 07.09.2014 – Proc. Pen. No. 1110/09 R.G.N.R. MOD. 21.
27 Proc. Pen. No. 1110/09 R.G.N.R. MOD. 21. Procura della Repubblica presso il Tribunale di Catanzaro, DDA. Fermo di indiziato di delitto, p. 40.
28 Ibid., p. 21.

References

Blok, A., 1988. *The Mafia of a Sicilian Village, 1860–1960: A Study of Violent Peasant Entrepreneurs*. Cambridge: Polity Press.

Cantona, R. and Di Feo, G., 2012. *Footballclan: Perché il calcio è diventato lo sport più amato dalle mafie*. Milano: BUR Biblioteca University Rizzoli.

DNA, 2016. Relazione annuale sulle attività svolte dal Procuratore nazionale e dalla Direzione nazionale antimafia e antiterrorismo nonché sulle dinamiche e strategie della criminalità organizzata di tipo mafioso nel periodo 1° luglio 2014–30 giugno 2015. Roma: Direzione Nazionale Antimafia e Antiterrorismo.

Romani, P., 2012. Coppola e Pallone: calcio e criminalità. In: Ciconte, E., Forgione, F. and Sales, I. (eds.). *Atlante delle Mafie. Volume 1*. Soveria Mannelli: Rubbettino.

Sergi, A., 2017. *From Mafia to Organised Crime: A Comparative Analysis of Policing Models*. London; New York: Palgrave Macmillan.

Sergi, A., 2016. Countering the Australian 'Ndrangheta: The Criminalisation of Mafia Behaviour in Australia between National and Comparative Criminal Law. *Australian & New Zealand Journal of Criminology*, 50(3) pp. 321–340 DOI: 10.1177/0004865816652367

Sergi, A. and Lavorgna, A., 2016. *'Ndrangheta: The Glocal Dimensions of the Most Powerful Italian Mafia*. London; New York: Palgrave Macmillan.

Vaccari, S., 2016. Relazione sulle infiltrazioni mafiose e criminali nel gioco lecito e illecito. In: *Commissione Parlamentare di inchiesta sul fenomeno delle mafie e sulle altre associazioni criminali anche straniere*. Roma: Camera dei Deputati & Senato della Repubblica–XVII Legislatura.

Chapter 6

Conclusion – mafia and Italian soccer

The state of the game

On November 17, 2017, Totò Riina, the '*capo di tutti capi*' (boss of the bosses) of the Sicilian cosa nostra, who ruthlessly led the clans during the '80s and '90s, died in hospital while serving several life sentences. The following is a transcript from the popular Italian satirical radio broadcast *La Zanzara* (the mosquito).[1] In this case, an undercover journalist randomly called the residents of the Sicilian town of Corleone, notoriously known as the Sicilian 'Mafia Town', to comment on the death of the cosa nostra boss:

UNDERCOVER JOURNALIST *(UJ)*: Good evening, Signora Riina.

- NB: The woman has the same surname of the boss – Riina – but does not have any family connections to him.

WOMAN (W): Yes?

UJ: Associazione amici Totò [Friends of Totò Riina Association] speaking; I am the president;[2] I wish to express our deepest sympathies . . .

W: Yes, but I am not interested to be honest.

UJ: Will you attend his [Totò's] funeral?

W: No, no! 'We' do not know anything.

- This reply is often used by the mafias' members; it is an expression of their code of silence (*omertà*) and repeated often (in other similar *La Zanzara* radio broadcast pranks) as some sort of automatic mantra by people who live in the territories where the mafia clans 'rule'. Totò Riina, arrested on 16 of January 1993 (*The New York Times* – online,

1993) followed the same script when, seven years later, he was interrogated by a public prosecutor: "I am an illiterate, Mr. Judge, and I'm afraid to confuse myself with words in Italian, I only speak [Sicilian] dialect; all my life has been in the [agricultural] fields, from morning to night; the mafia? I do not know what it is . . ." (*La Repubblica* – online, 2000).

UJ: But after all he [Totò] was not a bad person?

- Here the journalist continues his prank, pretending that the mafia boss was a very nice person, to see the reaction of the woman.

W: No, for me, he was a good person.

- The woman contradicts herself; now she knows who he is.

UJ: Back in the day[3] there were more job opportunities [irony]

- This statement is a constant of the undercover journalists of *La Zanzara*, who aim to uncover the social consensus – if any – enjoyed by the mafias (specifically cosa nostra, camorra, 'ndrangheta) in their regions of origin. It also reflects another of the many mafia myths[4] – part of their mafia *doxa* – namely that the mafia is seen as the resistance to the status quo of oppression and is just a group of 'knights in shining armour', as the myth of three Spanish knights, Osso, Mastrosso and Carcagnosso implies,[5] taking care of people otherwise abandoned by an inefficient and corrupt Italian state. The claim that the mafias offer job opportunities, regrettably, is true. To reinforce the myth of the 'Good Samaritans', but more importantly to maintain their grip on the territory, mafia clans find legitimate jobs for the unemployed or lend money without asking for it back. This 'unofficial' employment agency is also very active in soccer; as local soccer clubs are used to employing convicted affiliates, so soccer, as this book has tried to emphasise, becomes a formidable tool to produce social and political consensus.

W: Of course! Of course!
UJ: People were working more [irony].

W: We are not relatives though [statement to avoid being linked to cosa nostra].
UJ: However, Totò Riina has given us [Italy] visibility [ironic statement to elicit a response] in all the world; it's a classic example of 'made in Italy'! [irony]
W: He [Totò] was a person who worked as hard as any other person!
UJ: [irony] Eh yes, Signora, he worked very hard – a great worker – he was also very kind.

- Here, the journalist is once more provocative: In fact, Totò Riina was nicknamed 'la bestia' (the beast) for his ruthlessness against enemies (*Al Jazeera* – online, 2017). In 1992, he ordered the murder of judges Giovanni Falcone and Giuseppe Borsellino, and he killed hundreds of his opponents – one of his most heinous crimes was the murder of 13-year-old Giuseppe Di Matteo, January 11, 1996. Giuseppe Di Matteo was the son of repentant mafioso Santino di Matteo. Gaspare Spatuzza, another member of the clan who was collaborating with the Italian judiciary and police, stated that he kidnapped the 13-year-old boy, and after two years of imprisonment he was dissolved in acid to send a warning to those who might turn against Riina.[6]

W: Yes, of course! Even the relatives, the wife, all his family [are very kind].
UJ: OK Signora, thanks – again condolences, bye.

The transcript taken in isolation could be understood as a one-off, an easy way for *La Zanzara* to overgeneralise on the corleonesi (residents of Corleone).[7] In fact, *Sky News-Italy* (online, 2017) reported mixed comments of people of Corleone; among them there were comments of defiance against the mafia. One person, for instance, stated to journalists: "It would be desirable if with Riina's death mafia could also end, but I do not know if it will be so." Another interviewee underlined the importance of his arrest as the beginning of cosa nostra's end, even if he conceived that cosa nostra clans were still strong. Several Italian newspapers reported, though, the positive reactions in the social media which the newspaper *Il Giornale* (online, 2017) defined as a "Delusional Exaltation" of the boss nicknamed 'The Beast'. One post again stressed the (false) role of mafia as benefactor; the statement is chilling:

> You (journalists) can call him a killer as much as you like, but for some *palermitano* (residents of the major Sicilian city Palermo) he remains a hero because he helped so many families escape poverty, families with children who dreamed of a piece of bread at night. When he won public works contracts he gave jobs to many workers . . . so he did something good.[8]

While it is somewhat alarming that the support of mafia bosses in some regions may be seen as positive, data on the Italians' overall perceptions of mafias also are troubling. As mentioned in chapter 2, in 2017, a survey conducted by the Italian social research agency Demos demonstrated that one-third of the Italians interviewed perceive the mafias' power as stronger than 20–30 years ago; 46% stated that the mafia clans' influence remains unchanged, and only 2 out of 10 believed that mafia presence in Italy was diminished.[9] These results mirror the outcome of another important survey, this time carried out by the Law and the Economics and Statistics departments of the University of Palermo (Sicily). In March 2017, the researchers surveyed 800 university students in the Sicilian cities of Palermo, Trapani and Agrigento, and the majority of this highly educated 'sample' perceived mafia stronger than the Italian State and more dangerous than terrorism.[10]

Both surveys highlighted two points that this book has stressed in the past chapters – that although the phenomenon (mafia influence) is now strongly perceived in northern regions, which formerly were considered the less affected, in the southern regions mafia is perceived as totalising, affecting day by day the lives of the population.

It is in this milieu that the main difficulty lies in solving the long-lasting problem of the mafia, which is also interwoven with that of corruption. Bourdieu's frame, applying to mafia and corruption, has the merit to highlight their social dimension, which is fundamentally rooted in power exercise and maintenance via social consensus. As explained in our work, mafia and corruption meet precisely when mafia clans seek to exploit opportunities or become powerful through corrupt practices. The radio transcript from *La Zanzara* highlights the idea that to defeat both phenomena, collective action is the key strategy: any state repression – unless the social space changes – is always destined to remain ineffective.

In this book, we have aimed to highlight that soccer and mafia are 'fields' influenced by national and local power systems, which are – and are perceived by Italians as – highly dysfunctional, because corruption has become their main *doxa*. This depicts the diffusion and seriality of corruption-led practices in many fields of the Italian social space, including soccer; we believe it also depicts the extraordinary resilience of mafia in all its regional manifestations. In this social space, mafia power becomes normalised and, in the southern regions of the country, it superimposes upon the local corruption doxic power system, becoming at times difficult for the population to differentiate between what is legal and what is illegal. Mafia clans are so pervasive in some regions that their *doxa* is internalised by the population, promoting a widely accepted '*omertà*', expressed more often than not as normalisation, acceptance, consensus, as the woman interviewed by *La Zanzara* shows, and in other cases, fear. The problem of *omertà*, predominant in the south, was stressed in January 2017 by the chief constable of Naples, who explained that it had delayed the arrest of the camorra killer of 17-year-old Genny Cesarano, occurring in 2015 (*Il Mattino* – online, 2017).

It is by tackling corruption and mafia logics (*doxa*) and their impact on social actors' *habitus* that the problem might be significantly reduced. In Bourdieuian terms, it is crucial to promote hysteresis or a mismatch between the *doxa* of the field(s) and *habitus*. It is necessary to disrupt what Bourdieu (1989) identified as the comfortable ease of *habitus* in familiar fields: when this occurs, reflexivity switches on. This allows individuals to bring to consciousness what, for others, is taken for granted as they are pushed to analyse themselves (Grenfell, 2008). This forces the *habitus* to abandon its taken-for-granted orientations and to adopt more reflexive, calculated and hopefully ethical modes of operation (Bourdieu and Wacquant, 2007; cf. Bourdieu, 1977, 1998).

The disruption of the corruption-mafia *doxa-habitus* may be accomplished only via education, as the director of Transparency International-Italia explains:

> Education is a crucial tool; schools and universities should play an important role – their programs should stress ethics and the rule of law. This must be complemented by an anti-corruption education which targets the country's bureaucracy at local and national level. It's crucial to form the future leadership of the country in every field by promoting the importance of the common good rather than personal profit.[11]

In this book, we have argued that soccer, which is both a practice for social cohesion and a profitable business, is not immune from the attention of mafias at both the local and national levels and many steps in between, precisely because it has this duplex nature. Controlling soccer means gaining financial, social and political power, and in this sense, Italian soccer offers the perfect example of a field where power is vulnerable to wealthy and well-connected criminals but also corrupt(ible) entrepreneurs and/or politicians, both of whom share the willingness to acquire money and power.

As explained in earlier chapters, cosa nostra, camorra and 'ndrangheta have very similar *modus operandi* but also some differences in how they 'play' the power game and how they permeate societies and criminal markets. In the soccer field, we have many commonalities; cosa nostra, camorra and 'ndrangheta know the potential of soccer to increase their power as well as social and symbolic capital. Bruno Palermo, a Calabrian journalist and one of the exponents of the antimafia association Libera, explains the link between mafias and soccer this way:

> In Calabria (but also in other regions such as Campania and Sicily), soccer players – who are more famous and loved by fans – are often invited to birthday parties, Catholic baptisms, first communion days, confirmations and weddings. If the players know 'the

territory' or the soccer club, this provides the player with someone clued up (who knows which place or people are OK and which you should avoid) and everything will be fine. However, this does not always occur; the 'ndrangheta (and other mafia clans) relish in their power; their dominion on the territory is based on this *modus operandi*. If an important soccer player of the local soccer club attends a baptism of the daughter of a local 'boss', for the mafia 'boss' this means his power is recognised; the player thus becomes another symbol of status, prestige and power for the boss and the clan and any observer. The 'boss' would say 'I made this player attend the baptism'. However, there are players so silly who claim not to know the connection of the event to mafia; frankly I have difficulty in believing this naiveté. I think in many cases this might occur almost unconsciously; the reason is that in these locations saturated by mafia, people breathe mafia, they cannot avoid it and many times cannot say no. They attend the event to avoid their house being burgled or to avoid being 'shot in the legs' so they prefer to accept the invitations.[12]

In an attempt to advance recommendations for the lessons learned throughout the research conducted for this book, we can conclude by specifically looking at two aspects that need attention and reform when it comes to breaking the relationship between mafia-style corruption and Italian soccer:

1   Profiles of governance of the soccer industry
2   Lower divisions, amateur and local teams

The first is the one where interventions need to be agreed upon in the short and medium terms, as they relate to the industry and its shortcomings that make it more prone to mafia interests. The second is arguably more important from a perspective that looks at mafia power in the country but nevertheless is more about the nature of mafia power than it is about soccer.

1 Profiles of governance of the soccer industry

As for the first point, governance of the soccer industry is probably the aspect of the problem that includes the highest numbers of actors, beyond mafias.

All three mafias exploit the criminal hub of opportunities that Italian soccer provides daily. This occurs primarily because of the lack of accountability and transparency, especially of the youth and lower soccer divisions. As we have previously argued, mafias are a power from below – their penetration in society arises from below.

Moreover, Italian soccer can be said to be having a crisis, and this is not only because of the result of poor governance but also because of economic difficulties of the industry. Arguably, this crisis is also brought by a lack of talented soccer players. Ultimately, this crisis is reflected by the failure of the Italian national team to qualify – for the first time in 60 years – in the FIFA World Cup, which will be held in Russia in summer 2018.

As mentioned, the weaknesses of the Italian soccer field, especially poor accountability and transparency in the administrative and financial side of soccer management, are exploited by mafia power. Soccer provides mafias with fertile ground for accumulation of social, economic and symbolic capital to increase their status, respectability and social consensus. The accumulation of these capitals is not just what mafias want; it is also what other capable investors – both legal and not legal – might want. In this sense, corruption of Italian soccer happens – and gets normalised – before mafia power even infiltrates. However, the mafia method – intimidation, exploitation of *omertà* and employment of the associative bond to foster criminal reputation – can support the establishment and maintenance of a corrupt system, and, especially in soccer, it is employed by mafia groups and their affiliates as well as by 'normal' others, usually white-collar offenders.

As the governance of the soccer industry is indeed a business type of governance, considering the amount of money it generates directly and indirectly, vulnerabilities include first and foremost organisational matters – these range from the systems of accountability of teams to the transparency of transactions in the buying and selling of players, but more crucially to the regulation of leisure activities connected to soccer, such as betting or even live attendance of matches. As for the first point, the real issue with the governance of soccer, both nationally and internationally, appears to be linked to the appointment of managers, brokers and directors. They are those who will be closer to the players and can influence them and the team's performance. At times these are selected among former players, ideally allowing for those liaisons between players and criminal networks we discussed in chapter 4 to progress. Obviously, the soccer industry should be concerned about a more careful selection of people in managerial roles in teams all over the country, but especially when it comes to territories where mafia and corruption systems operate more distinctly, the absence of mafia links should be part of the selection criteria.

As for the second point, according to the several police officers and prosecutors we talked to, betting amounts to around 2 to 3% of the overall (legal) GDP of the soccer industry and 50% of the illegal one. As explained by Antimafia Prosecutor Alessandro Sorrentino[13] – lead prosecutor for 'Operation I Treni Del Gol' in Catania, Sicily – and demonstrated through Operation Dirty Soccer: "the great interest in the soccer industry is not just in the alteration of results and match-fixing, but it lies in the possibility of exploiting that match-fixing through betting." The bridge between the mafia field and the soccer field is in the world of betting, which develops from a fraud, the match-fixing, and from the information about the fraud that mafia clans and their 'friends' can control and sell as needed. This has been facilitated in the past 10–15 years by online betting – the internet has allowed the circulation of money linked to betting. Wherever money is, the mafia system arrives, so it would be imprudent to assume that in the world of online betting there is no supervision or control by the clans and those close to them with an interest in soccer. On a practical level as well, the changes in the offline betting system do not deter this match-fixing/betting method. In Italy in fact, the possibility to bet – and win – on a single match (with different regulations across different championships) has been substituted (since 2003–2004) by a system in which betters had to guess all 13 results of the Sunday matches in order to win. Obviously, the guessing of one match is easier than the guessing of 13 matches at the same time, and so is the fixing, thus allowing for more bets, a higher jackpot and different criminal opportunities.

This system has been considered responsible for the transformation of soccer into a 'source of income' for managers and presidents of the football clubs through match-fixing. As noticed by the prosecutors of Operation Dirty Soccer[14]

> This is the pathological consequence of the end of the old system, which has been turned into a system of betting on single matches and on events during the matches as well (i.e. number of goals). The temptation for the protagonists of that single match – especially when the match is free from other types of tension and particular objectives to reach within the championships – to try and profit from something they can effectively control has become very strong.

It's obvious that a radical reform of betting is needed, as this is the core of the illicit business opportunity. This also needs to be paired with the fact that the main professional football clubs in Italy are also listed in the stock exchange. Arguably, this leads to the emergence of illicit activities present in the world of finance as well, such as insider trading – the buying and selling of information related to companies.

Certainly, together with normative and financial regulation related to the accountability and financial transparency of the governance of soccer and the regulation of the leisure activities around soccer, we need to consider the implications of full-blown criminal activities such as money laundering that affect the governance of soccer as well. For example, it has been confirmed that sponsorships of teams, of individual players and of their merchandise are among the preferred methods for laundering money in the industry. With sponsorships of both Italian and foreign teams, mafia groups as well as corrupt entrepreneurs or politicians investing illegally in the soccer field have found a very easy way to launder money, according to the prosecutors in Catanzaro on Operation Dirty Soccer.

It seems indeed very easy to move money, once it has been labelled as sponsorship money, in a system that is poorly regulated and controlled. Evidently, when it comes to money laundering and to investments of proceeds of crime in the legal economy or through the banking systems, in Italy as abroad, mafia groups will behave, as every other criminal network will, on the basis of opportunity and the reliability of partners and by ensuring maximum safety for the operation. The mafia method and the mafia *doxa* in these criminal activities will be lost and therefore are more difficult to pinpoint from a law enforcement perspective. Indeed, when the direct (personal or financial) connections between mafia members or mafia interests and the soccer industry are not visible, it becomes extremely difficult to prove the indirect connections between laundered profits and investments in soccer. Investing and laundering money through sponsorships of soccer teams or merchandising can be purely financial – a calculation of benefit; it becomes a way of laundering money amongst many other ways, thus not special or peculiar to mafia power at all. When the connections are instead visible and more direct, then we might be looking at local scenarios where the investment in soccer is symbolic to the prestige of the clan or is a manifestation of specific preferences of mafia bosses on the territory.

Last but not least, it is paramount to understand how, in the governance of soccer, the role played by hard-core and highly organised soccer fans (Ultras) becomes crucial to finding yet another bridge between the soccer industry and mafia power. According to Antimafia Prosecutor Sorrentino, in fact, the management of fans is one of the '*entry points*' of mafia groups in soccer, essentially because the Ultras tend to develop subcultural traits very similar to the mafia ones. For example, in certain cities, Ultras develop mutual assistance mechanisms among themselves; they tend to use violence and intimidation against opponents; they clearly disrespect – and fight – police and law enforcement as these promote order in the stadium; they organise in hierarchical structures to control the stadium during matches; they might engage in low-level drug distribution and/or other criminal activities on behalf of others. As we are reminded by Prosecutor Elio Romano, "In soccer, different social actors can use the mafia method for different purposes"[15] and therefore can easily align with mafia groups' interests. The relationship between managers of soccer teams and the Ultras, during live matches for example, has proved to be a problematic one: the managers have at different times needed the Ultras for the control of the stadium or other businesses (not always legal), but among the Ultras can indeed be mafia members pursuing mafia interests, thus creating yet another bridge between mafias and the management of soccer teams.

At times, connections with mafia organisations emerge more clearly than others. On December 14, 2017, the Italian Antimafia Commission approved their latest report on mafia and sport. We read here about the latest scandal related to the 'ndrangheta interests in the Juventus F.C. in Turin:

> In Turin, the 'ndrangheta acts as intermediary and guarantor within the ticket touting handled by the Juventus Ultras, thus controlling the Ultras who were connected to some local clans. (. . .) At times the boss of the Ultras group is part of the clans directly, like in the cases of Catania or Naples; at times, like in the case of the Genoa, even though the link between common criminality and mafia criminality is not clear yet, the organisational features of the Ultras are similar to those of mafia clans.[16]

While violence in stadiums is often considered as a stand-alone issue, not necessarily linked to 'bigger pictures', the Antimafia Commission calls for a screening of Ultras through reporting mechanisms at the entry of the stadium to monitor personal connections and a securitisation of the premises – for example by establishing local detention units – to improve responses to (potential) violence. While securitisation and extra regulation might not necessarily be a long-term plan in this case and might have detrimental effects by increasing the animosity of the fans against security personnel, the call towards a more careful understanding of the mechanisms in which Ultras and mafia connections operate is definitely a fundamental starting point.

2 Lower divisions, amateur and local teams

The second general aspect that needs to be addressed is connected with the fact that mafias are powers from below. This means, as mentioned previously, that the local dimension of the relationship between mafias and soccer is the one that has to be targeted first when hoping to succeed at all in fighting mafia power. Indeed, while regulation of policies, management and financial transactions might increase transparency and accountability at the national level, the local level is where mafias thrive. So an approach against mafia power and mafia interests in soccer needs to move beyond the focus on money and look closely at the mafia *habitus* and its social manifestations. Mafias' interests in the soccer industry at the local level, as said, does not just fulfil a profit-oriented goal or a mechanism for the concealment of profits; soccer is both a fundamental social practice and the bargaining place, with politics and business actors in the same territory. Soccer is, for mafias, the ideal playground for both generating social and financial ties and maintaining social consensus; it becomes an instrument of power as well as an instrument of profit.

Attention to lower divisions and to local teams, therefore, needs to consider the density of mafia power, as this density is bound to make a difference in what local teams mean to mafia groups. In some southern regions, where mafia presence is denser, local teams are more likely to be an instrument of social prestige, a tool to foster social consensus, a means to gratify the clan members in society. In other areas, where mafia presence is less dense, investments in local teams are more likely to be in the form of sponsorships and, as said, become money laundering or mechanisms that certainly represent an attempt to appear 'clean' by investing in the legitimate economy. In both cases, investment in local teams can be a springboard to reach national teams, either by reinforcing the mafia group's reputation and power or by representing a source of income or re-investments of proceeds of crime.

At the local level, it seems difficult to argue for regulation and/or policies against the interests of mafias in soccer without actually targeting mafia power more generally. In fact, arguably, at the local level – especially in mafia dense territories – soccer is just another manifestation of mafias seeking power and profit through local businesses and social practices. There are, however, ways in which lower divisions and local teams could be better monitored to reduce mafias' penetration and influence both in the local, and eventually in their national, reach. For example, the lack of an effective *youth talent development* strategy in local teams shows a shortcoming of the soccer industry that puts the industry at high risk of mafia penetration. As mentioned earlier, if education is the long-term plan to fight corruption, then investing in the youth of soccer is a way to ensure that young people are not approached or exploited by – and do not adhere to – mafia or other systems of corruption. The lack of a youth development strategy can also be considered a reason why talents are missing or misrepresented at the national level; thus a strategy in this sense would benefit soccer as a national practice as well. As we are reminded by the antimafia investigators interviewed for this book, the lack of a youth talent development strategy is not only against the spirit of fair play and the promotion of soccer as a practice of social cohesion and belonging, but it is certainly exploited by illicit systems, including mafia actors. It is not uncommon, for example, for mafia groups or mafia-led corruption networks to buy local amateur teams for the sole purpose of seeing them lose in the match-fixing they have established. This is detrimental for the team and the players and certainly does not promote the fundamental ideals of sport practices. It also pushes towards the normalisation of practices of mafia patronage among players who wish to 'make it' in the field.

At the local level, as said earlier, soccer is an instrument to shape the public image of the mafia clan. The social capital offered by the involvement in soccer, i.e. the network of relationships useful and necessary to act in the soccer field, is what interests mafia clans, both in traditional and derivative mafia territories. The direct investments in soccer teams at the lower divisions or local levels by mafia clans are not corruption in themselves, but certainly they enable corruption and fraud in sport activities. At the local level, the soccer team can become an extended arm of mafia power and, as such, enable further corruption. Depending on the territory and the type of clan, this can happen either by *exploitation* – the clan will exploit the team or the players to fix matches and organise bets; by *camouflage* – the clan will use the team to launder money and, for example, create bogus trails of investments and sponsorships in the name of the team; or by *investment* – the clan will use the team to establish themselves as credible actors in the soccer field and progress further in investments – contracts, subcontracts or brokerage activities, for example – in the industry.

Countering all these diverse practices is not easy, as it requires (a) a local knowledge of both mafia power and social capital involved in the soccer industry and (b) a system of regulation of access to the soccer industry at the local level, which, however, is not dissimilar to the type of regulation needed in other legal economies. More specifically, in order to counter the penetration of mafia power in soccer at the local level, mechanisms to prevent mafia power from penetrating the legal economy more generally are needed. These mechanisms have been assessed and proposed throughout Italian history and range from preventative measures on the patrimony (the non-conviction-based seizure of assets, for example) to certifications in the public sector, aimed at ensuring that companies and sub-contractors in certain fields do not exhibit mafia links.

In conclusion, any antimafia mechanism aimed at protecting soccer needs to start from the local level and certainly must have a starting point – in the recognition that mafia power affects soccer in three different ways. First, a soccer team – especially when it wins – gives a positive image to a whole city or village. This represents an advantage for whoever owns the team or can affect it, at both the local level and, depending on the team, on the national platforms. In the soccer field, important people from the power field meet; participating in these meetings is crucial for those who wish to invest and to be perceived as 'clean' entrepreneurs, if not benefactors. Second, in the stadium, as noted by Prosecutor Alessandro Sorrentino in his report to the Antimafia Commission,[17] there are no social differences – everyone is the same when it comes to supporting a certain team; it is like a religious faith. This means that soccer brings together all social classes and therefore allows entry to different sources of social capital at the same time; this also includes and explains the mixing with the Ultras when needed. This is especially true at the local level and the lower divisions or amateur teams, where the links with the territory are most obvious and mafia clans participate in the social field. Third, and certainly not least, soccer represents an extremely profitable (illegal) economic channel: from money laundering to fraud; from sponsorships of national teams and players to ownerships and investments of amateurs and local teams; from betting to ticket touting; from selling of counterfeit merchandising to tendering for subcontracts at the stadium; and so on. All these sets of activities define, and depend on, the nature of mafia power, the territory in which this power originates and proliferate, and who interacts with mafias for their own benefit.

As alluded to throughout this book, Italian soccer is in crisis, and the crisis participated in by entrepreneurs, politicians, mafia members, players, management and fans, for different reasons. In terms of corruption, for sure, soccer is a 'field' that welcomes all kinds of illicit and unethical behaviours, both from mafia actors and from whomever adheres to logics of wealth and power accumulation through illegal means.

The unethical dimension of contemporary Italian soccer and its proved links to mafia clans, in particular the 'ndrangheta, is probably the gloomiest note on which to end this book, as they contradict completely the reasons why '*il bel calcio*' (the good soccer) has become part of the Italian identity throughout the decades. Nicola Gratteri, chief antimafia prosecutor in Catanzaro, Calabria, in a TV interview in November 2016[18] stated that if there was a political resolve, the 'ndrangheta could be defeated in five to six years; sadly, though, reality shows that Gratteri was somewhat optimistic in his statement.

As explained in the latest Direzione Nazionale Antimafia e Antiterrorism report[19] the 'ndrangheta is present in all the core sectors of the country, namely politics, public administration and the economy (areas this book has identified as national and local power fields); it seems obvious that mafia power will not be defeated by the police or by laws, and surely not by politicians alone. Social justice, good local social and welfare policies, and the mobilisation of people are crucial in this struggle, and what better than soccer to join this struggle against the status quo? Due to their popularity, soccer teams throughout history have shown they have the potential to be important symbols of resistance, social integration and identity; let's hope the Italian soccer establishment is able to show the way.

Notes

1 The programme is popular because the journalists are more able than other radio broadcasters to uncover Italians' vices and virtues – mixing trivial topics with serious ones such as corruption, the far right, racism and mafia, providing

Conclusion – mafia and Italian soccer 159

a sociologically interesting glimpse of Italian daily life; in this case the undercover journalist randomly calls the residents of the Sicilian town of Corleone, notoriously known as 'Mafia Town', to comment on the death of Riina.
2 The call is a prank; obviously the association does not exist.
3 The journalist refers to the period during the '80s and '90s when Totò Riina was free and leading cosa nostra, and the Corleonesi clan were among the most violent and ruthless groups ever to take control of the organisation.
4 In chapter 2 we focused on the myth that the mafias do not kill children
5 Cf. chapter 2.
6 This crime changed the perception of cosa nostra in Italy; Spatuzza underlined how this heinous crime dispelled the cosa nostra myth that children would never be touched in any mafia infighting. For more analysis, we refer to Bolzoni, A. and D'Avanzo, G. (2011). *Il capo dei capi*. Milan: Rizzoli.
7 When corruption and mafia are analysed within the Italian context, social scientists find themselves in a very difficult position to carry out a value free analysis without getting caught in being accused of overgeneralising or promoting unconstructive stereotypes about the social actors object of the analysis. In Italy, corrupt practices are widely diffused and in many cases normalised, and in some regions of the country the mafias have social consensus – often the clans are protected by some part of the population. These are, regrettably, facts and must be reported even with the risk of being accused of generalising and reinforcing (absolutely wrong) stereotypes, referring to populations who live in territories of high mafia density. In this book, what we aimed to accomplish was to document the observable and uncover the link between social space and individuals' internalization processes and concomitantly the reasons of any associations between widely diffused corruption, the mafias and the most popular Italian socio-cultural practice, soccer.
8 Totò Riina morto, sulle pagine Facebook dei familiari centinaia di messaggi di cordoglio: "È stato un grande uomo"; cf. https://www.ilfattoquotidiano.it/2017/11/17/toto-riina-morto-sulle-pagine-facebook-dei-familiari-centinaia-di-messaggi-di-cordoglio-e-stato-un-grande-uomo/3984616/
9 Cf. Demos report and data retrieved at www.demos.it/a01467.php
10 'Mafia più forte dello Stato, così la pensano gli universitari siciliani'; cf. www.adnkronos.com/fatti/cronaca/2017/03/24/mafia-piu-forte-dello-stato-cosi-pensano-gli-universitari-siciliani_mfkPEUtqwnSaJu7gD2476I.html
11 Excerpt 11 interview DM (2017).
12 Excerpt 20 interview BP (2017).
13 Interview of Prosecutor Alessandro Sorrentino by Anna Sergi, May 25, 2017, phone conference.
14 Proc. Pen. No. 1110/09 R.G.N.R. MOD. 21. Procura della Repubblica presso il Tribunale di Catanzaro, DDA. Fermo di indiziato di delitto, p. 22.

15 Interview of Elio Romano by Anna Sergi, Procura di Catanzaro, April 2017.
16 Cf. www.corrieredellosport.it/news/calcio/serie-a/2017/12/14-35564596/cos_la_mafia_si_infiltrata_nel_calcio
17 Relazione Audizione Commissione Antimafia, confidential document shared by Alessandro Sorrentino with one of the authors.
18 Gratteri: 'Se ci fosse la volontà politica, 'ndrangheta sconfitta in 5 anni'; cf. www.ciavula.it/2016/11/gratteri-ci-fosse-la-volonta-politica-ndrangheta-sconfitta-5-anni/
19 DNA report (April 2017), p. 10. Prot. 12720/2017/PNAA.

References

Al Jazeera-online, 2017-last update, Mafia Boss Toto "the Beast" Riina Dies at 87. Available: www.aljazeera.com/news/2017/11/mafia-boss-toto-beast-riina-dies-87-171117074408360.html [November 18, 2017].

Bolzoni, A. and D'Avanzo, G., 2011. *Il Capo dei Capi*. Milan: Rizzoli.

Bourdieu, P., 1998. *Practical Reason: On the Theory of Action*. Stanford: Stanford University Press.

Bourdieu, P., 1989. Social Space and Symbolic Power. *Sociological Theory*, 7(1), pp. 14–25.

Bourdieu, P., 1977. *Outline of a Theory of Practice*. Cambridge: Cambridge University Press.

Bourdieu, P. and Wacquant, L., 2007. *An Invitation to Reflexive Sociology*. Cambridge: Polity Press.

Grenfell, M., ed., 2008. *Pierre Bourdieu: Key Concepts*. London: Routledge.

Il Giornale online, 2017-last update, Esaltazione delirante sui social: "Viva zu' Totò". Available: www.ilgiornale.it/news/politica/esaltazione-delirante-sui-social-viva-zu-tot-1464514.html [November 19, 2017].

Il Mattino online, 2017-last update, Camorra, metà dei napoletani ha paura di denunciare i delitti. Available: www.ilmattino.it/napoli/cronaca/camorra_meta_dei_napoletani_ha_paura_di_denunciare_i_delitti-2221430.html [January 30, 2017].

La Repubblica-online, 2000-last update, "Mafia? Non so nulla Lavoravo nei campi". Available: http://ricerca.repubblica.it/repubblica/archivio/repubblica/2000/10/17/mafia-non-so-nulla-lavoravo-nei-campi.html [November 16, 2016].

The New York Times-online, 1993-last update, Italy Arrests Sicilian Mafia's Top Leader. Available: www.nytimes.com/1993/01/16/world/italy-arrests-sicilian-mafia-s-top-leader.html [July 6, 2016].

Sky TG24-online, 2017-last update, Morte Riina, le reazioni (contrastanti) dei corleonesi. Available: http://tg24.sky.it/cronaca/2017/11/17/toto-riina-morto-reazioni-corleonesi.html [November 17, 2017].

Index

agency vs structure 21, 23
Anti-Crime Central Directorate 26–27, 29–30

bankruptcy 72–73, 94
betting 1–2, 9, 20, 69, 73–74, 116–117; betting control agencies 77; camorra and 103; and fans 63; governance and 151–152; and match-fixing 122; and money laundering 102; and 'ndrangheta style corruption 135, 137; online x; Operation Dirty Soccer and 119; Operation Last Bet 68–69; *see also* Calcio-Commese (Soccer Bets)
Biagianti, Marco 89, 90, 101
Bourdieu, Pierre ix, 8–9, 11–12, 19–20, 146–147; and corruption 21, 33–37, 41, 43, 45; and scandals 60–61; *see also doxa*; field; *habitus*

Calabria 3–4, 7, 10, 29–30, 43–45, 78; Grande-Aracri mafia clan in 90–91; prosecution and 87, 158; soccer in 148–149; social embeddedness of mafia in 118; *see also* Dirty Soccer; 'ndrangheta

Calcio-Commese (Soccer Bets) 65, 85–87
Cameron, David (UK Prime Minister) 18, 59
camorra ix, 6, 8, 24–25, 27–29, 31, 148; *doxa* of 45; and *omertà* 147; as part of society 44; and *raccomandazione* 38; and soccer 92, 103–105; and social capital 42; and Ultras 70–71
Campania 6, 27–29, 78, 107, 123; *see also* camorra
Capuani, Nobile 1–2, 126
Caridi, Antonio (MP) 39
Carminati, Massimo 88, 111n2
Carraro, Franco 66
clientelism 37, 39
Codognotto, David 71–72
competition 2–3, 22, 26, 37
corruption viii–xiii, 1–12, 18–24, 57–58, 104, 117–118; Bourdieuian analysis of 33–37; the camorra and 31; conviction for 94; as *doxa* 92; investigations of 99–102; levels of 109–110; and mafias 146–151, 156, 158, 159n7; and networks 85, 86, 88; 'ndrangheta style 131–137;

practices of 37–41; Sicilian mafia and 27; and the state 41–42, 45–48; typologies of 71–78; *see also* Dirty Soccer; scandals
cosa nostra 8, 24–28, 30–31, 143–146, 148, 159n6; American La Cosa Nostra 31; and soccer 99–103; and social capital 42; terrorist strategy of 47
Cosentino, Nicola 28

De Dampierre, Eric 60–61
Demopolis 61–62
Dirty Soccer 116–118, 121–123, 137–139; Brindisi-San Severo match 123–125; Juve Stabia-Lupa Roma match 125–127; 'ndrangheta style 131–137; Operation Dirty Soccer ix, 7, 10, 118–121, 151–152
doxa 20, 33, 35–37, 77–78, 94–95, 147–148; corruption and 39–41; and honour and shame 50n24; and power field 43–45; and scandal 59–60
Durkheim, Emile 9, 58

economics 8, 10, 14, 138; and corruption 20, 22–23; and cosa nostra 27; and mafias 32–33; and networks 84–85; and power field 44–45; and soccer 150; and the state 46, 48
Eldense Soccer Club 1–2, 126

fair play 2, 59, 77, 156
fans 57, 63, 67, 73–75, 89–90, 100–102; Ultras 70–71, 97, 153
field 9, 33–37, 40–41, 50n23, 74–77, 147–148; and Dirty Soccer 117–118; and mafia's interests in soccer 92, 98, 151; power field 30, 39, 42–43, 45, 47, 61; scandals and 60–61
FIFA viii, 18, 59, 132; World Cup ix, 63, 66, 150
film 26, 31, 40
fraud 92, 120, 151, 156, 157; fraudulent bankruptcy 72–73; soccer fraud 119, 138; sports fraud 66, 86, 101, 122; vote fraud 87

Gabrielli, Franco (Prefetto) 5
Giuliani, Fabio 6
Godfather, The 26–27, 31
Goffman, Erving 2, 59–60
Gomorrah 27, 31

habituation 62
habitus 33–37, 39–40, 43–45, 49–50n22, 138–139, 147–148; of 'ndrangheta 128–131
honour 26, 29, 30–33, 43–44, 50n24, 135–136
Huizinga, Johan 2–3

immigration 5, 57, 67
interviews ix, 7, 12–14, 88, 93, 139, 145
intimidation 32, 69–70, 95–96, 104, 139
Italy *see* Calabria; Campania; corruption; mafias; Sicily; soccer

law 15n19, 46–48, 51–52n54, 72–73, 153; and *doxa* 35; fraudulent bankruptcy 72–73; judiciary systems 76–77; Law Rognoni 32; *see also* Dirty Soccer

mafias 24–25; Bourdieuian analysis of 33–37; Mafia Capitale network 88; national networks between soccer

and 84–86; as power field 41–45; and soccer 3–6, 91–98, 109–110, 143–149, 157–158; theories and practices regarding 30–33; *see also* Calcio-Commese (Soccer Bets); camorra; cosa nostra; 'ndrangheta; networks
Malinowski, Bronisław Kasper 25
match-fixing 57, 63–65, 74–76, 151–152; and the Calcio mafia style 88, 91–93, 101–102; *see also* Dirty Soccer
methodology 11–14
money laundering 73, 152–153
Morabito, Giuseppe 87
Movimento Cinque Stelle (5 Stars Movement) 19

'ndrangheta 1–2, 4–8, 24–25, 28–30, 41–45; the Calcio mafia style and 87–88, 91–92, 94, 96–98; and soccer 105–109, 148–149, 154, 158; and soccer corruption 128–131; *see also* Dirty Soccer
neo-liberalism viii
nepotism 37–38
networks 62, 84–91, 107; *see also* Dirty Soccer; relational model
Niceforo, Alfredo 31

Oliviero, Francesco 32
omertà (code of silence) 6, 32, 43–45, 93, 143, 147
Operation Johnny 4, 42

Pagliuca, Donato 105
Palermo, Bruno 43–44, 148
politics 148, 158; and the Calcio mafia style 83–85, 104–105, 110; and corruption ix, 23; *see also* field; *specific politicians*
Prestipino, Michele 88, 131

protection 26, 32–33, 89, 97, 99, 101; *see also omertà*
psychoanalytic theory ix, 6, 8
public officials 71–73; *see also* politics; *specific officials*

raccomandazione 37–39, 74
rational choice 21–22
relational model 22–23

sacred, the 9, 25, 43, 58, 60
scandals 7, 9, 18–19, 23, 57–61, 154; and the Calcio mafia style 85–87, 106–107; of Italian soccer 64–71; and Italian soccer style 61–64; Operation Last Bet 68–69; Passoportopoli (City of Passports) 67; public perception of 33; Rolex affair 66–67; Tangentopoli ix, 18–19, 37, 48n1, 61; *see also* Dirty Soccer
Scordio, Padre Edoardo 4
Sculli, Giuseppe 86–88, 92
shame 50n24
Sicily 24–27, 32, 41, 44–45, 78, 151; Palermo 47, 146; *see also* cosa nostra
simulation 2
soccer ix–x; and corruption 2–6, 71–78; governance and 150–154; Italian soccer scandal 7; Italian soccer style 61–64; lower divisions and local teams 154–157; and mafias 91–98, 109–110, 143–149, 157–158; national networks between mafias and 84–86; scandals of 64–71; soccer authorities 77; youth soccer 69, 71, 74, 77, 109, 150, 155–156; *see also* corruption; Dirty Soccer; fans; networks

social capital theory ix, 42–43, 156–157
social dramas 60, 71
social space 9, 19, 30, 33–37, 43–44, 61, 147; and *habitus* 78
sport 2; *see also* soccer
Sturzo, Padre Luigi 5

Tangentopoli ix, 18–19, 37, 48n1, 61
Transparency International 23–24, 41, 61–62, 74–76, 148
TV 27, 31, 61, 65–66

Ultras see fans
United Nations viii

Villar, Angel Maria 57, 60
violence 27–28, 31–32, 42–43, 69–70, 100–101, 131, 153–154

Weber, Max 12
World Bank viii

youth 44–45; *see also under* soccer